THE BIBLE'S TARE
AND
BLIND SPOT

THE BIBLE'S TARE AND BLIND SPOT

THE UNFOCUSED WORDS OF DOCTRINES AND THEOLOGIANS OF MAINSTREAM CHRISTIANITY'S DENOMINATIONS

Steven Iruthaya

iUniverse, Inc.
Bloomington

THE BIBLE'S TARE AND BLIND SPOT
The Unfocused Words of Doctrines and Theologians of Mainstream Christianity's Denominations

iUniverse books may be ordered through booksellers or by contacting:

iUniverse
1663 Liberty Drive
Bloomington, IN 47403
www.iuniverse.com
1-800-Authors (1-800-288-4677)

ISBN: 978-1-4759-4493-8 (sc)
ISBN: 978-1-4759-4494-5 (ebk)

Library of Congress Control Number: 2012914932

Printed in the United States of America

iUniverse rev. date: 08/28/2012

CONTENTS

INTRODUCTION

For anyone who wants to follow early Christianity, this is one of the best books you may ever read. If anyone socially follows Christianity or wants to keep Christianity for social reasons, this book will bother your heart.

Someone may wonder why this book talks about Christianity and its ideas. The reason is simple. As Christians, we know the log in our eye is the first we need to remove. I have belonged to the Christian faith since infancy. I have the right to remove the log out of the body of Christ as part of the body of Christ. "Your eyes are important to your body" is one of the sayings of Jesus. A faithful or knowledgeable Christian believes in the eye of the Christ. I may anger someone, but that is not my intention. I have the right to express my observations for the benefit of others. There are some gray areas among religions, and I carefully cross boundaries. I don't cross over them. It was done only to give the best picture possible.

If you ever wondered why Christianity has so many theologies or what scriptures are based on, you will find it out from this book. However, you also will find out what words and doctrines they are hiding and ignoring. You will find the keywords they ignored and hid and their meanings when applied to scripture. You will also find out about the twisted scriptures used by early Christianity to try to fit their own version of Jesus and who the scriptures really applied to. This book also talks about the importance of receiving and accepting the Holy Spirit.

A lot of Christians forget to realize we have a two-thousand-year history. Many prophecies have already been fulfilled, but why are they only applying them to today's Christianity. You will very briefly explore early, middle, and modern Christianity's doctrines in this book. Your faith or general idea of Christianity's doctrines will change after reading this book. This book will have a very strong impact on your faith. It definitely breaks your old faith.

Before you read this book, answer some questions. Who is important to you—church, God, or religion? Which one would you choose? Who is powerful? Who should you listen to?

In the religious world, there is always a problem with those who want us to gain souls. Religious leaders or preachers brainwash their followers. Many are brainwashed from childhood. They were brainwashed by their religion. Their religion made them believe they are the only ones going to heaven.

The religious leaders say many things. Do you have to believe them? I was involved in a temporary business for a relative of mine. She traveled to India from Sri Lanka (Ceylon). In Ceylon, cloves are very expensive and known for their quality. The best cloves in the world are from Ceylon. In India, they can be sold for double the price. She was inexperienced, and it was her first time doing this business. There are always crooks in business. She bought cloves from one of them. She arrived in India. She gave me the cloves and asked me to sell them for her.

I took the cloves to a big store in town. The owner was a good friend of mine. He had known me for two years. He took the cloves and spread them over the table to check the quality. There were unwanted and unfamiliar wood pieces in them. He showed me. He did not buy them from me because of the quality. He rejected them because he knew I was inexperienced. He knew I was a good person. He rejected them because he did not want his customers' food to be bad because of the product. He showed me how to check them for the next time. He was a smart man. He protected his customers and his store.

In today's religious world, gaining souls is encouraged. People are asked to bring new souls to their groups. When you check their doctrines and ask them questions, everyone ignores their followers with many techniques. Everyone carries other people's doctrines and theology. Those who work to gain souls, do they check them? Or were they brainwashed over and over if they request their doctrines? Are they asking God to help open their eyes toward doctrines? The worst part is everyone becomes brainwashed. The followers who try to bring souls have to brainwash someone else.

What did we do with the cloves? I went home with the cloves and explained what had happened. We stayed overnight and spread the cloves on the table. We picked up every good piece and removed the bad pieces. I sold them the next day. I could have taken the mixed cloves to different stores and fooled a buyer by selling them for a cheaper price. There are people who do these things. They claim it is okay because they were fooled by someone else.

In business, if you are correct and bring pure quality, you may lose a lot of money—especially in the gold business. Many people are not willing to do the right thing because they may lose a lot of money, time, etc. People do not want to correct their mistakes because they are embarrassed.

In the clove story, we did the right thing. We spent the time to correct our mistake. It lost its original weight. What is the right thing? We took out the good pieces and did not sell the bad pieces. How many of you are willing to check your religion's theology or doctrine? What would you do if they were wrong? When I point out what is wrong, people call me bad names. Some blame me and say I am breaking up the church and faith. It was the other way around. I am trying to bring you blessings and show you how religion leads you away from those blessings. I am trying to protect you from blasphemy against God. I am helping you check your faith. People who are afraid to change their faith blame me.

Many church supporters are angry with me. Terrorists threaten the political system with religion and harming physical bodies. My writing is for your souls. We all die. It is about whether you die with sin or without sin. It is about you dying without blaspheming God. My writing is for your eternal life—not for a short period of time.

CHAPTER 1

BAPTISM

Repent and be baptized, every one of you, in the name of . . .
—Acts 2:38

According to Christianity, people are not Christians without baptism. According to the Bible, there is one baptism, one spirit, and one body with Christ Jesus. There are many baptisms in today's Christianity. Catholics usually are baptized as infants. Their godparents promise to guide them toward Christianity. They never make any promises for the baptism. However, they renew their promise unofficially.

Catholic priests usually ask bystanders to renew their promises when they baptize infants. How can anyone renew a promise that they never made? Even popes never made a promise to get baptized. Why do Catholics renew their baptisms? Did their baptisms expire? Are they going to expire? Catholics are so into godparent theory—even if a seventy-five-year-old grandpa wants to become Catholic, he needs a godparent. He never makes any promises.

A godparent's promise and how baptism renews promise are different. Officially, a Catholic never takes baptism with a promise or a renewal of original baptismal promises. One of the problems in Christianity is the name to be used since the Bible points out there is only one baptism for a Christian. As far as I know, there are three types of baptisms. Jehovah's Witnesses do not use any name during baptism. Two other types use different names. Pentecostals baptize in Jesus's name only. The other name using baptism is well known to all. Catholics baptize new Catholics using the Father, Son, and the Holy Spirit based on Matthew 28:19.

Catholics and Pentecostals claim it from the Bible. Who is using the right name in baptism? Catholics claim they are using the right name according to the Bible. According to Catholics, that is one baptism Paul wrote on his letter and others baptism are heretics. Catholics are condemning others, believing in the wrong baptisms, and practicing unacceptable baptisms.

Are Catholics using the right name in baptism? No, they are not. Why are they baptizing with the wrong names? Catholics claim Jesus instructed his disciples to use the right name as Jesus did in the Bible. Did Jesus really say that? We have no proof of what really happened. In order to understand what is wrong with the name and who is using the wrong name during baptism, we need to take look what he said and who he gave those instructions to.

Eleven disciples went to the mountain in Galilee to which Jesus had directed them. When they saw him, they worshipped him—but some doubted.

> All authority in heaven and on the earth has been given to me. Go therefore and make disciple of all nation, baptizing them in the name of the Father and of the Son and of the Holy Spirit and teaching them to obey everything that I have command you. (Matt. 28:16-20)

Jesus was asking his disciples to teach them to obey. Did the disciples obey Jesus? Did they baptize in the Father, Son and the Holy Spirit? No, they did not. Jesus was ordering or giving instructions to his disciples. Disciples had to follow instructions from the master. If they were not followed, something was wrong with the disciples. They were following someone other than the master. None of his disciples ever baptized anybody with the Father, Son, and the Holy Spirit. Peter and John did not baptize anyone with the Father, Son, and the Holy Spirit. Paul did not baptize anyone with the Father, Son, and the Holy Spirit. The Bible does not end with Jesus commanding his disciples before he departed.

There are other books in the Bible that detail what happened after Jesus departed. There are descriptions of how Jesus's disciples worked after he went to heaven. None of them indicated if any of his disciples baptized anyone with the Father, Son, and the Holy Spirit. This only appeared in Mathew as Jesus commanding his disciples. The Bible did not end there; it continued with baptism stories at least seven times.

Even after Jesus commanded his disciples to baptize new Christians in the name of the Father, Son, and the Holy Spirit, they ignored him. They ignored their own master. There is no proof this formula was practiced by early Christians anywhere in the Bible. It has never been used. Since it was not practiced by early Christians, what name were they using to baptize new Christians? They were using Jesus's name to baptize new Christians. Since the Father, Son, and the Holy Spirit were unpracticed and appear in one verse, it is under suspicion. Did Jesus really say it? Maybe Jesus never said it. There was a problem with Corinthians. They started to divide among themselves. Paul asked every strong question about baptism, and he was asking what name they were baptized with. "Has Christ been divided? Was Paul crucified for you? Or were you baptized in the name of Paul?" (1 Cor. 1:13).

The answer is not written for this question, but we all know the answer is no. They were not baptizing in the name of Paul. We have to ask why Paul was asking about the names. Paul was trying to tell the Corinthians they were baptized in Jesus's name. He was asking who had been crucified. The same name was used in baptism. The Father, Son, and the Holy Spirit were not crucified. Jesus was crucified. If this is not directly involved enough, look where Jesus's name was used to baptize.

> "Peter said to them Repent, and be baptized every one of you in the name of Jesus Christ'" (Acts 2:38).

> "They had only been baptized in the name of Lord Jesus" (Acts 8:16).

> "Then he (Peter) ordered them to be baptized in the name of Jesus Christ" (Acts 10:48)

> "On hearing this, they were baptized in the name of the Lord Jesus" (Acts 19:5).

Paul, Peter, and John were involved in baptizing in Jesus's name. John and Peter were with him in the mountains when he gave instructions. Why did they disobey him? How could they preach someone that they disobeyed? It is clear they were not using the name of the Father, Son, and the Holy Spirit. Only Jesus's name was used in baptism. "I baptize in the name of Father, Son, and the Holy Spirit" cannot be used.

When the first gentile converted to Christianity, it was a Roman general (Acts 10). After he received the Holy Spirit, Peter ordered them to baptize in the name of Jesus. When Paul baptized John's disciples (Acts 19), he used Jesus's name. He put his hand on the disciples and they received the Holy Spirit.

In early Christianity, they did not only baptize in his name. They also cast out the devil in Jesus's name. They performed miracles in his name.

> "Master, we saw someone casting out demons in your name" (Luke 9:49).

> "In the name of Jesus Christ of Nazareth, stand up and walk" (Acts 3:5).

> "This man is standing before you in good health by the name of Jesus Christ of Nazareth" (Acts 4:10).

> Many will say to me on that day "Lord." Lord, did we not prophecy in your name, and in your name cast out demons, and in your name perform many miracles? (Matt. 8:22)

There was no incident if anyone cast out devil, cure sick, perform miracle in name of the Father, Son, and the Holy Spirit.

> This Jesus, There is salvation in no one else, for there is no other name under heaven given among mortals by which we must be saved. (Acts 4:11-12)

In early Christianity, the apostles preached that salvation and power would be given only by Jesus. In Acts 4:11-12, Peter was talking to a high priest about salvation. No other name is given—that includes the Father, Son and the Holy Spirit. There is no evidence of anyone casting the devil in the Father, Son, and the Holy Spirit.

The Bible has an introduction about every book by denomination, including the gospels. They explain who wrote it, what language it originated in, and what language it was going to be translated to. In most cases, it was translated from Greek. A few denominations want people to know it originated in Hebrew.

When I researched Wikipedia about the Gospel of Matthew, I found out Bishop Papias of Hierapolis translated the Gospel of Matthew into Greek. He is one of the church fathers and saints. Papias wrote about the Gospel of Matthew and pointed out it was originally in Hebrew. He translated the best he could. He introduced the Gospel of Matthew into Greek in AD 100-140. The copies they have now are from Greek. All copies in Greek might have originated as papyrus. He was not the best translator, but he translated as best he could. No one has the original copies of any gospels or Paul's letters. The copies of the gospels and Paul's letters are carbon-dated to AD 200. Mathew 28:19 is a later inserted by someone else. The Gospel of Mathew we read today is translated from Greek—not from Hebrew. It was believed to be written in Hebrew by Bishop Papias (http:en.wikipedia/wiki/ Gospel_of_Matthew).

If you want see how Papias made translation errors, look at Matthew 21:7. It is not possible as described in Matthew. The story is about Jesus entering Jerusalem. It proves the translator or early interrupters were not masters in translation. "They brought the donkey and colt, and put their cloaks and he sat on them" (Matt. 21:7).

No one really cares about these kinds of mistakes. It does not belong to any doctrine. Everyone agrees that Matthew 21:7 has translation errors. Mark gives you the right picture. You cannot sit on two chairs beside each other. According to Matthew, he sat on two donkeys.

Someone on the Internet claims to have a copy of the Gospel of Matthew in Hebrew. I am not sure how reliable or honest this claim is. I don't know if they have done any carbon dating. If what he claims is proven, Matthew would say, "Go baptize in Jesus's name" (http://Juese-messiah.com/apologetics/Catholic/matthew-proof.html).

Jesus preached many things with parables so even uneducated people could understand. He made it easier for them so they could see things in their daily lives.

> The kingdom of heaven may be compared to a man who sowed good seed in his field, but while his men were sleeping his enemy came and sowed tare among the wheat, and went away, but when wheat sprouted and bore grain, then the tare became evident also. (Matt. 13:24)

If I explain the moral of the story, I have look through my experience. My maternal grandparents were involved in farming. I was with them in my early teen years. We had a rice field. In a rice field, some kind of grass is grown with it. Both look the same in the early stages. In the early stages, nobody touched it. When they grew, the rice looked lighter, and the grass looked darker.

We removed them from the edges. If it was in the middle and we spotted it, we couldn't go into the field because we may step on them and destroy the rice. A day or two before cutting the rice, we hired experienced laborers or asked experienced neighbors to help remove the bad crops. Unless you take a close look at it, it is unnoticeable. Both crops would look healthy. When you realize bad crops are growing, you realize they will need to be removed. Even if the problems were noticeable, we couldn't do anything until the right time came.

According to the parables, Jesus said the devil sowed tare in God's field. This also applies to the Bible. A few insertions were removed by Catholics because they believed it was tare. However, they have not removed every tare.

The other moral of the story is the unwanted grass crops bore seeds and spread faster than the rice. Of course, it would spread kill the good crops. It would occupy a lot of land and have no use for anything. It would take up our land where we could grow wheat.

In Jesus's parables, there is tare in God's field. Let him know what the owner decides to do with what is in his field—or let him tell us what we should do.

CHAPTER 2

JESUS'S GENEALOGY

Hosanna! Blessed is the one who comes in the name of the Lord! Blessed is
the coming kingdom of our ancestor David!
Hosanna in the highest heaven!
—Mark 11:10

Some of the problems in Christianity are Jesus's birth and Jesus's genealogy. Christianity places more importance on his birth stories than his genealogy. Why is his genealogy more important than his birth? Almost all Christians preach and believe Jesus was born of the Virgin Mary. Only a few Christians do not believe it. It is their individual belief. As church doctrine, all of them believe it. Islam has similar beliefs. A lot of Christians don't understand why Jesus's genealogy is important to Christian faith. A lot of Christians do not know Jesus was not born of a virgin. Belief in the virgin birth destroys an important part of Jesus's genealogy. Before looking at why Jesus's genealogy was important, let's look at what is wrong with the virgin birth story.

Matthew 1:-23 points out an Isaiah prophecy. "Look, theVirgin shall conceive and bear a son. And theyshall name him Immanuel." However, it has a huge mistake. I assume the mistake was made by someone who rewrote the gospel.

Bibles after 2011 point out Isaiah 7:14 as an exact translation. They changed it from virgin to a young woman. In fact, there was a translation error in Isaiah 7:14. Many were changed thirty years ago to put the correct word. Catholics changed it thirty years ago. King James was changed in 2011. It is no longer there. It is no longer in anybody's Bible. It remains unchanged in Matthew. Even though they changed it, it does not apply to Jesus or Mary. It does not even apply to any future king. There is no connection to Jesus. There is no connection to Jesus as Immanuel. The prophecy in Isaiah 7:14 never fit Jesus.

Then Isaiah said: "Hear then, O house of David! Is it too little for you to weary mortals, that you weary my God also? Therefore the Lord himself will give you a sign. Look, the young woman is with child and shall bear a Son, and shall name him Immanuel. He shall eat curds and honey by the time he knows how to refuse the evil and choose the good, the land before whose two kings you are in dread will be deserted. The Lord will bring on you and on your people and on your ancestral house such days as have not come since the day that Ephraim departed from Judah—the king of Assyria." (Isa. 7:13-17)

Do you know a prophecy has a time line or deadline? When Peter denied Jesus, Jesus prophesized the event. A rooster was pointed out to identify the time. In fact, the rooster's crow was used to indicate the time.

Isaiah's prophecy is similar to the rooster prophecy. It has time and it has an end time. King Ahaz feared his brother in Israel and the Assyrian superpower who joined Israel. Israel was divided into two after King Solomon. Judea was the southern kingdom of Israel, but it was called Judea. Because Ahaz was obedient to God compared to other wicked kings, God sent Isaiah to Ahaz with a promise and a sign. He will destroy the enemies of Judea. Woman was given as The sign who was with King Ahaz. "Young woman is with child." Her child's life is the time line of the prophecy. "Look!" This is how Isaiah started his prophecy. He was pointing to a woman with a big belly in the king's palace.

Therefore, the Lord is bringing up against it the mighty flood waters of the River, the king of Assyria and all his glory; it will rise above all its channels and overflow all its bank; it will sweep on into Judah as a flood, and pouring over, it will reach up to the neck; and its outspread wings will fill the breadth of your land, o Immanuel. (Isa. 8:7-8)

Everyone knows Immanuel means "God with us." God is with Judea—not with Israel.

But a man of God came to him and said, O king (Amaziah), do not let the army of Israel go with you, for the Lord is not with Israel—all these Ephraimites. Rather, go by yourself and act; be strong in battle, or God will fling you down before the enemy; for God has power to help or to overthrow. (2 Chron. 25:7-8)

God asked his prophets to name their children. Prophet Hosea codenamed his children. Why was he codenaming his children? In Isaiah 8:3-4, he is giving his own children a code name to identify Israel's future. In the prophecy, a child's name was used as a code name. It was normal in the Bible. Immanuel is a code name—just as Isaiah's children's names were given by God as a time line.

This story has nothing to do with Jesus. Jesus was born under Roman rule. Even in Jesus's time, the Assyrian kingdom didn't exist anymore. It had already been overcome by the Babylonians. There were no kings threatening Judea or Israel. God never promised a virgin birth. It was the opposite—a promise made to King David. His sons would be on the throne forever. It was called an unbreakable promise. It was like steel, you are not able to break it. God's promise is better than steel. It is unbreakable.

A wicked queen ruled Judea for a short period. She decided to destroy the promise that God had made to King David. She decided to kill all the king's children. She killed all but one. How was that child saved? Joash was hidden by his aunt. The aunt was the king's daughter and sister. She was not killed. She was never hidden. Her house searched for the king's child. It proves only male members were considered as King David's descendants to the throne. She never hid any of her children. It was not from the daughter of King David. His mother's name was mentioned when they identified kings. The wicked queen story she did not find the child. When this child become a king at age seven or eight, the wicked queen was killed. The high priest made this child a king (2 Chron. 23:3). "Here is the king's son! Let him reign, as the Lord promised concerning sons of David".

Do today's Christians have any idea what David has to do with Jesus being the Messiah? A lot of Christians do not understand the first sentence of the New Testament. What does it mean? Why is it there? Christians don't have a clue. The first subject in the New Testament is about Jesus's relationship with King David. And Jesus as ruler of the kingdom.

Matthew's first sentence and first subject is about Jesus, the son of King David. Jesus's kingship is more important to Jews because he has the right to rule. The New Testament contains at least four hundred pages. No one cares what the first sentence is. Why would an author want that to be his first subject about David's son? Why do Christians want to start the Bible with this sentence? Why would Peter preach at the beginning of Christianity that Jesus is the son of King David? In fact, he was preaching that after received the Holy Spirit. No one cares about first day of Christianity or the first sentence of new testament of the Bible.

It is important to accept Jesus as messiah. It is not possible without accepting him as the son of King David. Peter and Paul were trying very hard to prove that Jesus was the son of King David.

> "Follow Israelites since he (David) was prophet, he knew God had sworn with an oath to him that he would put one of his descendant on his throne" (Acts 2:29-30).

"God made David their king. In his testimony about him he said, 'I have found David, Son of Jesse, to be a man after my heart, who will carry out all my wishes. Of this man's posterity, God has brought to Israel a Savior, Jesus, as he promised" (Acts 13:22)

"Remember Jesus Christ raised, from the dead, a descendant of David—that is my gospel, for which I suffer hardship, even to the point of being chained like a criminal."

This is not someone swearing an oath. It is God swearing an oath. Have you ever promised something to someone? What does it mean? No matter what happens—you going to keep your word. The promise is for King David's sons. It is never for any of his daughters. That is why you do not see a list with women's name on it.

I am able point out more from Paul's letters. Jesus was preached by Paul. There were lots of arguments about his relationship to King David. Many Christians are not denying Jesus is the Messiah. In fact, they blame Jews for not accepting Jesus as the Messiah. According Christians, Jews do not know anything about the Messiah.

Christianity and Islam believe that Jesus is the Messiah and came from a virgin birth. I am not sure if Islam knows the Messiah has to be King David's son. Christians have different beliefs. They believe Jesus is the Messiah according to the oath God made to King David, but it is through the Virgin Mary daughter of King David. Someone claims luke genealogy list of Jesus is different and belongs to Mary. No! The Bible never said that. It is not a list of Mary. The list belongs to Joseph. It starts with Joseph and his fathers and his fathers. All of them are male names.

"As was thought" in luke 3:23 possibley inserted by someone who introducing the virgin birth to Christians. "As was thought" then why bother continue with Josephs father's list. Why couldn't Luke give a list of Mary's fathers? Matthew never has "as was thought" on his list. Matthew and Luke are trying point out the list from Joseph. How can they deny Joseph as father? Even though both of them contradict each other, all the names are males.

A man on the Internet said, "Now Sheshan had no sons, only daughter; but Sheshan had an Egyptian slave, whose name Jarha. So Sheshan gave his daughter in marriage to his slave Jarha; and she bore him Attai" (1 Chron. 2:34). He claimed the Bible points out a descendant can continue from a daughter.

First of all, in Jesus's birth story or genealogy, there was no claim of David's son not having a son. It said that Sheshan has no sons. It is solid proof that only male descendants are counted. The Bible gave male slaves names, but Sheshan's daughter's name is never given. Jarha and his wife had a son—and his name is given. Someone easily buys this verse and says it is proof. But it proves the opposite.

I have questions for the ones who believe Jesus came from the Virgin Mary. What does the Messiah mean? What is he anointed for? Where in the Bible does it say God promised his Son? Where in the Bible does it say he would send a virgin? The promise was clear for King David.

> As Jesus went on from there, two blind men followed him, crying loudly "Have mercy on us, Son of David!" Then he touched their eyes and said "According to your faith let it be done to you." And their eyes were opened. (Matt. 9:27-29)

CHAPTER 3

JESUS'S FAMILY

Did Jesus have brothers and sisters? There are two beliefs in Christianity about Jesus's brothers that were mentioned in the Bible. Pentecostals believe the names mentioned as Jesus's brothers are half-brothers. Catholics believe they are his cousins. Where do these beliefs come from?

Pentecostals believe the Virgin Mary was the second wife of Joseph. There is no proof in the Bible. After Jesus, she had two sons and a daughter. Catholics believe Joseph was only married to Mary. Jesus was born through a virgin birth. All the other people mentioned were cousins. And they claim the translation changed it to brothers. And they also argue that one of the names on the list had the same name as his father. Joseph cannot name his father. Jews do not give their father's name to a child. Therefore, it is not the same family. Catholics also claim they were not half-brothers or brothers.

"Is not this the carpenter, the son of Mary and brother of James and Jose and Judas and Simon, and are not sisters here with us" (Mark 6:3).

"Is not this the carpenter's son? Is not His mother called Mary, and his brothers, James and Joseph and Simon and Judas" (Matt. 13:55).

In Mark and Matthew, the name of one brother was seen by Catholics as different. Which one could be the real name of that brother? Is it Jose or Joseph? I think it is Jose.

Jews have a tradition of naming their children after the father. According to the Bible's famous birth stories, Jesus's birth story is fictional. Maybe Jews do not have that tradition as Catholics claim. If they believe in birth stories, it is not possible.

Now the time came for Elizabeth to give birth, and she bore a son. Her neighbors and relatives heard that the Lord had shown his great mercy to her, and they rejoiced with her. On the eighth day they came to circumcise the child, and they were going to name him Zechariah after his father. (Luke 58-59)

I hope you understand the birth story is about John the Baptist. The prophet who introduced baptism before Jesus is not John the Buddhist. He is John the Baptist. Is he a Jew? Are his relatives Jews? Yes. Jews wanted John to have the same name as the father, but it did work out. Therefore, the Catholic argument no longer fits. What are Catholics going to say now?

Is that name for half-brothers? Maybe not. Let's see why. The word half does not appear there. The Bible was careful in naming the father of some apostles—especially when they have the same first names. Since Jesus is the main topic, would they mention their mother's names?

Today we have TV and entertainment; in those days, the neighbor's life was entertainment. Have you lived in a community without TV? Does your neighbor's life compare to the old days? If your neighbor had two wives, would you know it? I had that experience; my neighbor was the second wife. One of first wife's kids and second's wife kid and I are the same age. We played together. If any one of them was to be reported, we used their mother's name to identify them. This was more practical.

When people in Jesus's city told him, we know he would mention his half-brother. The authors have a responsibility to point that out. Have you ever taken your brother's or sister's kids with you? How would you introduce them if you met one of your old friends? You would properly tell your friend who your kids are and who are your nieces or nephews. In one conversation, we properly introduce family members. The authors in the Bible did not feel that much responsibility? Why are there certain verses in the Bible that may not make sense? You want to take them literally. Why don't you take this one literally? The Virgin Mary story won't fit. One of them has to be taken as tare and be removed. Christianity chose to take Jesus's family as tare. This is the real wheat that needs to be respected. The Virgin Mary story is the tare.

Catholics ask, "If Jesus had a brother, why would he give his mother to John on the cross?"

> Meanwhile standing near the cross of Jesus were his mother, and his mother's sister Mary (?), Mary (?) the wife of Clopas, and Mary (?) Magdalene. When Jesus saw his mother and disciples whom he loved standing beside her, he said to his mother, "Woman, there is your Son (?). Then he said to the disciples, "Here is your mother" and from that hour the disciples took her into his home. (John 19:25-27)

Do you get the picture here? Four women were standing close to the cross before Jesus died. All of them had the same name: Mary. There was no main point in the picture by the author. The author did not say one of his disciples was standing among the woman. He also did not mention that he was there too. The word in the chapter was changed for some unknown reason. Jesus's disciples ran away from him as prophesized. No male disciples were there.

That picture also did not fit in with the other gospels. The gospels said, "Women were from Galilee, stood at a distance" I think this makes sense; the disciples got scared and feared for their lives. That is why the gospels indicate the women were looking at Jesus's death, including John's Gospel. The women did not want see a killing. Many women do not want to see animals being killed for food. That is why they were at a distance—not very close. There is also a reason Jesus's mother was never there. Jesus didn't say said that was in John 19:26. Everything in the gospel did not end. It continued with the apostle and Mary. We can find out what happened to Mary. Where was she? Who was she with?

> All these were constantly devoting themselves to prayer, together with certain woman including Mary the mother of Jesus and as well as his brothers. (Acts 1:14)

If they were cousins, why is Jesus brothers with Mary? Why were they not with other mothers? If there was another mother of Jesus's brother, why did they not write her name? In the previous sentence, the author wrote everyone's name in detail. The next verse is careless. I think he was carefully writing Acts 1:14 as he wrote Acts 1:12-13.

What was wrong with Jesus's crucifixion according to the Gospel of John? Jesus carried his cross by himself (John 19:17). No one helped him. In another gospel, Simon and a Roman soldier helped carry the cross. Both cannot be true.

There was no proof Jesus ever carried the cross. Another gospel said, "Then they led him away to crucify him" (Matt. 27:32, Mark 15:20). Jesus probably never carried his cross. The Roman soldier carried the cross at first and Simon carried it for them after.

Catholics have Stations of the Cross. Jesus fell with his cross three times—even after Simon carried the cross. If Simon or the soldier was carrying his cross, how could he fall three times? At least two other times, he didn't carry his cross. There is no mention of Jesus taking his cross from Simon.

According to John, he carried the cross by himself—and only John says women are close to him. How close to the cross? All the women were standing around and he was talking to his male disciples. The Gospel of John crucifixion story is cannot be true if we believe the other gospels' crucifixion stories. All Christian writings, gospels, and Paul's letters indicate Jesus had a brother.

CHAPTER 4

MARRIED APOSTLES
AND DISCIPLES

Were Jesus's disciples married?

As a Catholic, I wanted to be priest. Catholic priests do not marry. In my early teens, I took it seriously. I started reading religious books and the Bible. I never focused on the subject every time I read about marriage. Whoever get baptized is a disciple of Jesus. That is why Christians baptize new Christians. Can God's servants marry? I had to deal with myself during my late teen life. Catholics believe Peter was the only one of Jesus's disciples who married. That is not true. Almost all of them were married and lived married lives.

"Do we not have a right to take along a believing wife? Even as the rest of the apostles and brothers of the Lord and Cephas" (1 Cor. 9:5).

Who was asking this question? Paul's question sounded like he was married. He was talking about other apostles taking their wives when they were traveling to do God's work. Who else married? The rest of the apostles. Who are those rests of the apostles? Everyone married—even after Jesus poured down the Holy Spirit on them. Why did they have wives? What Jesus said contradicts what the apostles were doing. In Matthew 19, Jesus was saying something different.

> For there are eunuchs who were born that way from their mother's womb; and there are eunuchs who were made eunuchs by men; And there are also eunuchs who made themselves eunuchs for sake of the kingdom of heaven. He, who is able to accept this, let him accept it.

If that is for the kingdom of God, why didn't his disciples live alone? They married. The problem was they had to bring their wives with them. Why does a man need a wife? A woman can be brought as a server. The argument was about bringing a wife. What Paul really complained about was the other apostles were having happy nights with their wives while he was having lonely nights while he traveling for God. The problem was more about sex. It was not about whether they were allowed to marry or not.

As a Catholic, I used to believe the subject was whether they were allowed to marry or not. The subject is different. It's about lonely nights. Because of above code word, I did not believe Jesus really said anything about eunuchs. Someone added it later.

Why didn't I accept one of Jesus words? According to Mathew, the above words were the last words Jesus said after discussing divorce. They only appear in Mathew. The same subject was in Mark, but eunuchs do not appear in Mark. In Mark, it was nice and practical. After speaking about divorce, Jesus blessed the children.

> Have you not read that He who created them from the beginning made them male and female for this reason a man be joined to his wife, and the two shall become one. (Matt. 19:5-6)

If Jesus was telling his disciples not live a married life for God's kingdom, why didn't they follow it after they got the Holy Spirit? They were married—and they even made Paul jealous about their happy nights. Paul's complaint was strong evidence the apostles lived with their wives and had sex with their wives.

Many of God's servants were married, according to the Bible. Isaiah married a prophetess. God wanted Hosea to marry an unfaithful woman. These were God's servants living married lives. God is the one who wanted them to marry a particular woman. Most of the prophets were married. Jeremiah had grandchildren. Were they not God's servants? They were serving God. If it was for the kingdom of God, why didn't they stay unmarried?

God allowed all of his servants to live married lives. God made them for each other—to be joined with each other.

The Lord Jesus said, "God has joined together, let no one separate them" (Mark 10:9).

CHAPTER 5

SCRIPTURAL THEOLOGY
AND THE HOLY SPIRIT

*My Lord Moses stops them! But Moses said to him, Are You jealous for
my sake? Would that all the Lord's people were prophets, and that the Lord
would put his spirit on them!*
—Numbers 11:29

There are two beliefs in Christianity about the Holy Spirit. A majority of them believe the Holy Spirit is a person. Catholics, Pentecostals, Anglicans, and others share these beliefs. And others do not believe the Holy Spirit is a person (Jehovah's Witnesses and Jews). Christians claim it originated with the Jewish religion, but they never believed the Holy Spirit was a person.

Do you know your church's official doctrine of the Holy Spirit? Do you know what scripture they were based on? Many who believe the Holy Spirit was a person have no idea what their own beliefs are. There is an official belief that many of denominations work under. They believe the Holy Spirit is proceeding from the Father and Jesus.

There is no question among anyone about the Father's spirit. There is a question if it proceeds from Jesus. In the Catholic Church, order to proves that he proceeds from Jesus they read John 20:22. After Jesus resurrected, he appeared to his disciples while Thomas was not there. Before he departed, he blew on the apostles—and they received the Holy Spirit. Thomas was not there. He did not receive the Holy Spirit. "When he had said this, he breathed on them and said, Receive the Holy Spirit" (John 20:22).

When did Jesus's disciples receive the Holy Spirit? In Acts 2, Jesus received the Holy Spirit from the Father and poured it down on his disciples on Pentecost. How many times did they receive the Holy Spirit? Is it while he was on earth? Is it forty days after he departed earth? According to the Gospel of John, there was a reason why he went to heaven. The reason was so he could send the Holy Spirit

Nevertheless I tell you the truth: it is to your advantage that I go away, for if I do not go away, the advocate will not come to you: but if I go, I will send him to you. (John 16:8)

There is no other writing claiming this except the Gospel of John. Jesus gave the apostles the Holy Spirit while he was on earth. Did his disciples receive the Holy Spirit while he was in heaven or while he was on earth? John 20:22 and John 16:8 contradict each other. The Gospel of John contradicts other New Testament writings. When do you think Jesus gave his disciples the Holy Spirit?

Don't blame other denominations if you don't have an official written theology on the Holy Spirit. How do you know your denominations are not using the wrong scripture or ignoring words in the scriptures? New emerging Christian groups blame other denominations, but they don't have an official document stating their beliefs and what they are based upon.

The Bible discusses his spirit, Father's spirit, and God's spirit—it always uses a singular pronoun. There is no "our spirit" or "their spirit." It never uses the plural. The Bible claims the Holy Spirit only proceeded from the Father.

Is God the Holy Spirit or is the Holy Spirit the spirit of God? Which one is right? Both cannot be right. There is also a problem of how the Holy Spirit is identified. Some Christians identify God's spirit and others identify God the spirit. Both have different meanings.

God the spirit is the wrong idea. Only God's spirit is right. That is what the Bible says.

"For it is not you speak, but the Spirit of your father speaking through you" (Matt. 10:20). Can we say Father the spirit as we are saying God the spirit? If the Bible is written by people who have the Holy Spirit, they never write God the spirit. They have only written as the God's spirit. Also even with the Holy Spirit in them, they never write in the plural. Who do you trust?

Language problems play a big part in the Bible and doctrine, especially when it comes to the Holy Spirit. The Bible was written in Hebrew and Greek. Some books of the Bible were translated into Greek from Hebrew. In Jesus's language (Hebrew), there is no word for "it."

"I cut it (tree)" does not exist in Hebrew. Possibly, "I cut her" exists (directly translated from Hebrew). "I cut her" can be misunderstood. Someone could easy assume you murdered your wife or a woman. The sentence is not much of a translation problem if translated into Greek.

"It is very dark" does not exist in Hebrew. Possibly, she is very dark exists (Hebrew).

In Greek, there is pronoun for "it," but the word has to end with the feminine or masculine. "She is very dark now" (Hebrew) would be confessing to a translator. A translator may use "she" without understanding the subject. How would you translate it? "She" needs to be replaced with "it." Every translator would not understand it right. "She is very dark." "It is very dark." It sounds like a woman has dark skin.

It was dark cloud day when I was writing this. Yes, I was talking about when the apostle and Jesus spoke, but language has a pronoun "it." The Holy Spirit has translated language to language, spoken Hebrew to written Hebrew, and then to Greek in Jesus's time.

Today's English is the main language among nations that communicate with each other. In English, to fill a gas tank, they say, "Fill her up" Even though English has better grammar than Hebrew and Greek, people use them differently.

After AD 200, Christians started to write in Latin. In 2000, the Bible was translated from Greek to English. It was translated from English to other languages. Translators have trouble since both languages are different. That is why sentences play important roles. The few sentences need to be read carefully to understand the subject. Is it for those who already have understanding the subject? If a translator has problems understanding the ideas surrounding a subject, he may end up translating wrong. There are the Bible translators who do take advantage of it and are used by some churches to fit their theology.

Some people claim the Holy Spirit is a person. They question those who say the Holy Spirit is God's force. Will the force speak? Maybe not. If you hear someone speaking to you, it is not the person you hear—it's a person's voice you hear. People have voices in their throats. The force in the throat becomes a voice. A voice is not a person.

Where is the voice after someone stops speaking? Your ear received a voice. If you are not deaf, you will hear them. A speaker needs to be able to produce a force through the throat (there are mute people who can produce that force). A person who hears it needs to have enough force in his ear to hear the voice. Maybe a force can't speak, but it makes you to speak. It makes you hear a voice. (Breath of the mouth also can be translated as spirit of the mouth).

Many preachers point to the Bible to prove the Holy Spirit is a person and God. It is separate from God. After Ananias sold his land, he took a part for himself and gave the other part to the church. Peter called him and asked him about it, and he lied.

"Why has Satan filled your heart? To lie to the Holy Spirit and, you did not lie to us but to God" (Acts 5:3-4). You lie to the Holy Spirit and you lie to God. They draw the conclusion that Holy Spirit is God and a person because he hears the lie. God filled his heart with the Holy Spirit, but what is Satan's heart filled with? There are other problems.

When did Ananias lie to the Holy Spirit? Did not Peter call him? Did not Peter ask the questions? Peter is talking to him. In conclusion, Peter is the Holy Spirit.

Peter did not say, "You lie to me, liar." The person who is speaking is Peter—not the Holy Spirit Person. Peter heard the lie. The early church controlled by power of God's force. They had dreams and they heard voice inside them. God was telling them what to do. That is what it means. Possibly Peter heard a voice ask what is Ananias up to. Your voice is connected to you in the same way the Holy Spirit is connected to God. It would make sense. If you take it directly, you lie to us—but God can interrupt. Peter makes himself as the Holy Spirit and then he makes him as God.

There are stories in the Bible about miracles that did not involve people at the point of miracles.

> "God did extraordinary miracles through Paul, so that when the handkerchiefs or aprons that had touched his skin were brought to the sick, their diseases left them, and the evil spirit came out of them" (Acts 19:11-12).

> "She came up behind Jesus and touched the fringe of his clothes, and immediately her hemorrhage stopped" (Luke 8:44).

> "Man was thrown into the grave of Elisa; as soon as the man touched the bones of Elisha, he came to life and stood on his feet." (2 king 13:21)

We understood there are miracles the Holy Spirit or God's spirit was involved in. These are the examples where a piece of cloth cured the sick. Why is there no doctrine on it? Jesus turned around, but the woman didn't touch him at all. She touched a little bit of his clothes.

The Holy Spirit controlled the church during early Christianity. Annis never lied to the Holy Spirit, but he did lie to Peter. However, it was understood to be lying to God. There is no direct logic used in this conversation. Do you know you can receive the Holy Spirit in an amount?

"Then the Lord came down in the cloud and spoke to Moses, and took some of the spirit that was on him and put it on the seventy Elders" (Num. 11:25). God took some spirit from Moses and gave Israel seventy elders. "Some" is an amount. He took and put into seventy elders. "Took" is an amount. No matter what translation, there was an amount involved directly or indirectly.

Some Bibles describe the first martyred Stephen "full of" the Holy Spirit. "Full of" is an amount. Full of spirit that his body (soul) could take.

Elisa said "Please let me inherit a double share of you spirit" (2 Kings 2:9). Did Elisa ask for a double share? Is it possible to have a double share? You could have a double share of a person's property. You couldn't say, "Send your double son with me" It does not make sense. The Holy Spirit is not a person. Can you receive a person in "double,"

19

"some," "full of," or "same as?" No, you cannot. Somehow all of these words disappear when they are preaching and on their doctrine. No one would ask questions because they are on stage. People are too shy to stand up and ask questions. They think it is inappropriate to ask questions in front of others.

Peter points out the difference between God and the Holy Spirit.

"No prophecy ever came by human will, but men and woman moved by the Holy Spirit spoke from God" (2 Peter 1:21). What does this mean? While they were filled with the Holy Spirit, God spoke to them. Who is ignoring the Holy Spirit? Many churches claim the Holy Spirit is a person. They don't realize an important person cannot be ignored. A lot of people didn't understand it.

Kate Middleton and Prince William married on April 29, 2011, in England. Many people were invited. Who was invited? Regular people? No! Kings, rulers, and famous people. When there is an important event, important people are invited, according to their own customs.

For example, the king and queen of Denmark needed to be invited by Prince William's father. Charles maybe sent an official with an invitation—not by phone or letter. I do not know their customs of inviting. If William's father did not invite a king and queen just one sea away, there would be few sides to that story. It would be Charles denying fatherhood of William. He did not know the right manners. Charles would look like a bad person or Denmark would have a bad ruler. England would not believe in Denmark's existence.

This example is important. A person needs to be properly invited—and not ignored. The Holy Spirit was ignored by Jesus when he spoke about eternal life, last day, etc. Why would Jesus ignore a person?

> "This is eternal life that they may know you, the only true God, and Jesus Christ whom you have sent" (John 17:3).

> "But about that day and hour no one knows, neither the angels of heaven, nor the Son, but only Father" (Matt. 24:36).

Does the Holy Spirit know the end of days? Why is the Holy Spirit ignored? Can someone like Jesus ignore the existence of an important person? I can point out many verses like these. These two are important: eternal life and end of days. If that is not enough, when John wrote who is the antichrist, he ignored it

"Who is the liar but the one who denies that is the Christ (Messiah)? This is the antichrist, that one who denies the Father and the Son" (1 John 2:22). Why did John ignore the Holy Spirit? How about a person who denies the Holy Spirit? John was denying the importance of the Holy Spirit when he was speaking about the antichrist.

Christians who speak in tongues not claim the Holy Spirit is speaking through them. They all say we received the Holy Spirit and speak in tongues. I want to know what "received" means to them. These people support the Holy Spirit as a person.

Why is the Holy Spirit not a person? What does God's spirit mean? We all have a spirit. It is a human spirit. However, no person has a human spirit. If I am speaking to another person, he has the human spirit—and I have the human spirit. The human spirit is not a person.

Do we have a human father? Yes, we do. Do we have human spirit? Yes, we do. We have a body. What happens to life in it? We are dead. To be living, we need to have our own spirit. To be human, you need to have a human spirit. Human spirit is in every human being. Is a human spirit a person? Without human spirit, there is no human.

In Daniel 4, God gave King Nebuchadnezzar the mind of an animal—and his human mind was taken out of him. He behaved like an animal for seven years. Every animal has its own spirit. God gave them certain abilities. Even a worm has spirit. Every living being has a spirit. Without that spirit, they do not belong to a particular family.

> Thus says God, the Lord, Who created the heavens and stretched them out, who spread out the earth and what comes from it, who gives (living) breath to the people upon it, and spirit to those who walk in it. (Isa. 42:5)

The Bible says the Holy Spirit is the Spirit of God. King Nubu talked to Daniel. King Nubu had a dream that no one in his kingdom declared the interpretation. He said, "You are able, however, for you are endowed with a spirit of the Holy God." Daniel was reviled by the dream—not by the human spirit. He was able to interpret because he had God's spirit.

Many humans can solve our own problems. Do you think young children don't have human spirits? Humans behave differently. They can't deal with adult situations. What do young kids do? They go to school, learn, and prepare to become grownups. In the Bible, it says people with the Holy Spirit are called children of God. It also says God gave us his own spirit.

> For if you live according to the flash, you will die; but if by the Spirit you put to death the deeds of body, you will live. For all who are led by the spirit of God are children of God. For you did not receive a spirit of slavery a spirit of adoption. When we cry, "Abba (Father)," it is that very Spirit bearing witness with our spirit that we are children of God. And if children, then heirs, heirs of God and joined heirs with Christ." (Rom. 8:13-17)

A person with the Holy Spirit will call God "Father." He gave you his spirit as spirit of his own.

> Therefore I want you understand that on one speaking by the Spirit of God ever says "Let Jesus be cursed!" and no one can say "Jesus is Lord" except by the Holy Spirit. (1 Cor. 12:3)

People who have the Holy Spirit will call God "Father" and say "Jesus is Lord." What did the apostles tell the children of God to call the Holy Spirit? Nothing! Some pointed out the spirit gave gifts as the Spirit chose. How is that possible if it is not a person? God gave the Holy Spirit to a person.

God will send the Holy Spirit to a person. The Holy Spirit is not going to a person by itself. God has to put it. God has to allow it. The Holy Spirit does not allow what power needs to be active in a person. As a person receives the spirit, it becomes a separate issue. That is why spirit chooses to apply, but spirit does not give a gift.

God gives his own spirit as a gift—he makes the decision. With human spirit—some are doctors, lawyers, or bus drivers. Who decides that? Human spirit. The human way of living. Some are in college or university. What serves the human race for a profession? It is part of human spirituality—the same way a person who acts on his own according to the spirit that he received from God.

Islam also is included in this subject. Worse than Christians, Islam has many groups and many different beliefs. There are two main groups. According of them, the Holy Spirit is an angel, and Gabriel is a person. Both main Islamic groups agree the Holy Spirit is a person. An angel has the Holy Spirit, but it's given to them. The Bible describes the difference between the Holy Spirit and an angel. There is a story in the Bible of the first gentile convert. He was a Roman general who worshipped the Jewish God. He was not Jew—he was uncircumcised.

> In Caesarea there was a man named Cornelius. One afternoon at three o'clock he had a vision in which he clearly saw an angel of God coming in and saying to him "Cornelius." He stared at him in terror and said, "What is it, Lord?" (Acts 10:1-4)

He saw an angel. The angel ordered it to get Peter. Peter came to this man's house and preached to the general. The general and his people received the Holy Spirit.

> While Peter was speaking, the Holy Spirit fell upon all who heard the word. The circumcised believers who had come with Peter were astounded that the gift of the Holy Spirit had been poured out even on the Gentiles.

The general "saw angel" and "received the Holy Spirit." This is very clear. The Angel and the Holy Spirit are not the same. The Holy Spirit is not an angel. An angel is viewable, and a spirit is invisible. Islam never speaks about receiving the Holy Spirit. This is one major difference between Islam and Christianity.

In Christianity, they speak about receiving the Holy Spirit. Islam never talks about receiving the Holy Spirit. Islam claims Christians are far from Jewish beliefs. Jews don't pray to receive the Holy Spirit, but Christians do. Many people fake and act like they have received the Holy Spirit. That is a problem. Christians are not far from Jewish beliefs. Jews are far from their own beliefs.

Today, Jews do not receive the Holy Spirit, but early Jewish Christians did practice it. The coded word comes after the title of the Torah. So it is not pagan idea. Islam can no longer say Christians receiving the Holy Spirit is a pagan idea. (Please do not ignore the word receive).

I wonder what Jews say on the subject of receiving spirit. When Abraham was called, he was uncircumcised—and he was prophet for a long time without circumcision. He had one son before he was circumcised. God can give the Holy Spirit to the uncircumcised. Abraham is the best proof.

How did Christianity move from receiving the Holy Spirit to worshipping the Holy Spirit? I was discussing Christian history with a pastor. He accused me of speaking history. Somehow the discussion ended. I wondered if I was talking history. Was I talking Christian history? Was I speaking about the Macedonian Empire or Alexander? No. I was not. He took Christians out, it sounded like I discussed something unimportant. Is Christian history not important to Christians? Is it important to Hindus? Buddhists? Jews? Islamists? But not for Christians? I won't bore you with a long story. I will briefly tell you Christian history concerning the subject. History can be found in Wikipedia and you can Google it, if necessary, for more detail.

Catholics has prayers for the Holy Spirit. Other denominations claim they could request the Holy Spirit to come upon them. There is no proof in the Bible. The Bible has subjects about receiving the spirit. The Bible says, "If you received a different spirit from the one you received, you submit to it readily enough" (2 Cor. 11:4). Do you know the date of this warning? Can you guess?

How does the Holy Spirit need to be worshipped in Christianity? In AD 380, history was important. People had the wrong beliefs. According to Catholics, there was a heretic named Macedonius in AD 360. Macedonius said the Holy Spirit should not be worshipped. Why did Macedonius proclaim it? Some Christian groups joined with Rome in AD 325 to become the official religion of Rome. It broke.

Other Christian groups called Arians took power, and they broke. Pagans ruled Rome. In 350, Macedonius had different beliefs. He said the Holy Spirit did not need to be worshipped. Bishop Athenians said the Holy Spirit needed to be worshipped. There was official agreement with Rome about Christian beliefs and what they were allowed to preach in the Roman Empire. He preached the Holy Spirit needed to be worshipped. However, worshipping the Holy Spirit was not part of the agreement. He did it without consulting anyone or any church.

In 380, Catholics took back power and met with the last king of Rome, Thodus 1. They announced Macedonism was heretical and punishable by law. They also said the Holy Spirit is proceeding from the Father and the Son. If there is no Macedonius, the Holy Spirit will not proceed from the Father and the Son. He may not be worshipped. He proceeded from father and son and took them 400 years. After AD 400, the Holy Spirit is proceeding from Father and Son.

Many Christian denominations work under the same theology. Somehow, they blame Catholics, but they don't have the official scriptural documents.

In 325, some church fathers agreed with the Roman king. The agreement was only about beieving the Holy Spirit. This is incomplete and confusing. What was supposed to be believed was not there. Do I believe in receiving the Holy Spirit? Is it wrong? When I point out this section of Christian history, some argue it was from the Apostles' Creed and the church fathers modified it. The apostles did not have a creed. Paul, in his letters, warned about different doctrines, but he never gave advice to any one of his group to follow the Apostle's Creed. Why? Because they didn't have it. If he had it, would he advise them to stick with the creed? (The Apostles' Creed is a name given in the fifth century. It was not from an apostle.)

Moses wants God's people to receive the Holy Spirit. He wants all of them to become prophets. All the prophets wanted God's people to receive the Holy Spirit. God also wants you to receive the Holy Spirit.

> Two men, one named Eldad and other Medad, had remained in camp; yet the spirit rested upon them. They were among those recorded, but they had not gone out of the tent. And they had spoken in ecstasy (Prophesied) in the camp. A youth ran out and told Moses, saying, "Eldad and Medad are acting the prophet in the camp!" And Joshua Son of Nun, Moses' attendant from his youth, spoke up and said, "My Lord Moses, restrain them!" But Moses said to him, Are you wrought up on my account? Would that all the Lord's people were prophets, that the Lord put His spirit upon them! (Number. 11:26-29-Torah/bible)

CHAPTER 6

How to Receive
the Holy Spirit

If you then, who are evil, know how to give good gifts to your children.
How much more will the heavenly Father give the Holy Spirit
to those who ask him!
—Luke 11:13

Christians has to rely on the word "receive." Why is this important for Christianity? Early Christians preached many things. If you accept Jesus as Lord and Savior, you will receive the Holy Spirit as gift. Why is this so important? Let's say you met a very rich man. He showed all of his wealth and his servants. He was wealthy and happy. Then he sent you home. You start your regular life. What is point of seeing that man? He was proud of himself—what are you proud about? You can only be proud about what you have. I cannot be proud about what someone else has. If you're Christian, that is what you have to get from God for accepting Jesus. That is why Christianity is different from other religions. You have the right to get the Holy Spirit and become children of God.

In this chapter, we are going to see why God is giving his spirit to Christians. Who would receive the spirit? How can you receive the spirit? What purpose is given? Who will receive the Holy Spirit?

"And so is the Holy Spirit who God has given to those who obey him" (Acts 5:32). God gives the Holy Spirit to those who obey him. Here is another word "obey." God blessed Abraham in his father's house. God asked him to move. He did not challenge him. He did not say God blessed him. I will stay here and enjoy my life with my brothers and my family. He chose to obey and moved far away. It was not an easy decision. Abraham chose to relocate without challenging God. He worked with God's plan. He did not ask God to change God's plan. God saved Nova from a big flood.

For God, the one who obeys him is more important than the whole world. It means if you do not listen to God—you are on your own. God cares for and helps those who obey him. A person who is obedient is important to God. God will share his plans. If they obey him, they don't need worry. It is not politics—the majority wins. A television pastor explained how we are a minority on earth, but we are the majority in the universe. God has uncountable angels. If the majority on earth obey God, it is good. One is better than nothing. Nova's story proves he saved Nova among all people because of his obedience. "But, as written what no eye has seen, nor ear heard, nor the human heart conceived what God has prepared for those who love him" (1 Cor. 2:9).

Paul wrote about God's spirit of adoption. Christianity was God's plan.

There are only two notable methods to receive the Holy Spirit in the Bible.

> God gives it directly: "While Peter still speaking this word, the Holy Spirit fell upon them" (Acts 10:44).

> It is given through God's man: "When Paul had laid his hand upon them, the Holy Spirit came on them" (Acts 19:6).

Some people who received the Holy Spirit also have the gift of giving the Holy Spirit to others. This needs to be noticed. A person who obeys God not only gets the Holy Spirit; he can also give it to others.

> Now when the apostles at Jerusalem heard that Samaria had accepted the word of God, they sent Peter and John to them. The two went down and prayed for them that they might receive the Holy Spirit. (For as yet the Spirit had not come upon any of them; they had only been baptized in the name of the Lord Jesus). Then Peter and John laid their hands on them, and they received the Holy Spirit. Now when Simon saw that the spirit was given through the laying on the apostles' hands, he offered them money. Saying, "Give me also this power, so that anyone on whom I lay my hand my hands may receive the Holy Spirit." (Acts 8:14-19)

Simon wanted the gift of giving spirit to others. He did not ask for negative things. He asked for the right thing—and the good thing. Peter, Paul, and John had that gift but no other apostles did.

Peter said, "Because you thought you could obtain God's gift with money, your silver perish with you" (Acts 8:20).

The only way of getting the Holy Spirit is by obeying God. The Holy Spirit only comes through obedience to nothing but God.

Why should you receive the Holy Spirit? To do his will and his work. People with the Holy Spirit are called children of God. They are obeying God and doing his will. They are called servants of God for the same reason. In some cases, they are called prophets. A prophet preaches about God and brings people closer to God.

Should women receive the spirit of God? Yes. The promise of the Holy Spirit was never only for men. Everyone points out men who receive the Holy Spirit and their stories. There are hidden stories of woman who were prophetesses. Woman prophesied future events. Prophets write sometimes—and sometimes they hire someone to the do the writing for them.

Some women did not have financial abilities or education in those days. In today's world, uneducated people read at least a newspaper or finish some studies in childhood. We are living in an educated world compared to other ages. Their lives were not discussed because they did not deal with problems in society. Maybe they explained what they saw or what they dreamed. Maybe they did not preach.

> God declares that I will pour out my spirit upon all flesh, and your sons and daughters shall prophecy and your young men shall see visions, and your old men shall dream dreams. Even upon my slaves, both men and women, in those days I will pour out my spirit; and they shall prophecy. (Acts 2:17-18, Joel 2:28-29)

> "He had four unmarried daughters who had the gift of prophecy" (Acts 21:9).

> "But any woman who prays or prophesies with her head unveiled disgraces her head" (1 Cor. 11:6).

> "Prophetess Huldah the wife of Shallum; she resided in Jerusalem in the Second Quarter, where they consulted her. She declared to them, "Thus says the Lord" (2 Kings 22:14).

In order to have God's spirit, women don't need to be virgins. Covering the head indicates those rules for married women. According to their customs, they respect the head of the house.

God promised he would give his spirit to women. No one was allowed to stop God's will. Who are we to stop God's will? Covering the head with a veil shows respect for men. For some cultures, respecting the men is different. Were they allowed to follow their rule according to their tradition? I do not want to go into the subject of women's clothes or how they dress. God gave them, he would give them, and he promised he would. We should respect God's discussion if we are obeying God. Women can have the Holy Spirit because God wanted them to have it.

Don't assume the Holy Spirit is free as some scriptures say. The Holy Spirit is not for sale—but it is not free. In order receive the Holy Spirit, there are rules. The simple rules are based on obeying or repenting God.

There was king before King David. He was anointed by Samuel. He name is Saul. He was a prophet. And he received the Holy Spirit. But He lost it. Why did he lose it? He worked with his own plans.

> As you come to the town, you will meet a band of prophets coming down from the shrine with harp, tambourine, flute, and lyre playing in front of them; they will be in a prophetic frenzy. Then the spirit of the Lord will possess you, and you will be in a prophetic frenzy along with them and be turned into a different person. Now when these signs meet you, do whatever you see fit to do, for God is with you. (1 Sam. 10:5-7)

Why did he lose it? There are very basic rules—you cannot go to another God. If a person is possessed by other gods or devil spirits, you cannot get help from them. Don't ignore God's ability help you.

CHAPTER 7

TWISTED JESUS AND REAL JESUS

According to the prophecies, who is Jesus?

As a Christian, I have to believe in Jesus. The fact is we never see Jesus. There are so many doctrines about who Jesus is. We never see the apostles. We do not believe someone who is king and ruled some country that is visible on TV or a computer. Many believe Jesus will return to the earth after almost two thousand years.

Why is believing in Jesus important? According to the Bible, God gives the Holy Spirit to those who obey him. Christianity begins with receiving the Holy Spirit. God wants Christianity to exit as his kind. Many Christians claim they have the Holy Spirit. According to early Christianity, when you accept Jesus, you receive the Holy Spirit. Accepting Jesus is real challenge based on the doctrines that are available today. Christianity is still valid—the promises remain the same as two thousand years ago. We know God gives the Holy Spirit to those who obey him. Accepting Jesus, we obey God or God's future plan. That is why we are receiving the Holy Spirit.

What are the beliefs about Jesus? You may have heard Christians saying Jesus is God, and God the Son is first creation of God. There is Jesus's nation—the Jewish people—who do not care about it. They also reject Jesus as Messiah or anointed ruler of Israel. Some Jews agree he may only be prophet. Islam agrees he was the anointed king of Israel. Islam also has another belief Jesus is an angel.

Who is Jesus according to scripture—and proclaimed by his apostles—and what are they pointing out? Many churches would agree with whatever scripture says. Are they pointing out the right scriptures? Is something wrong with the scripture they are showing? Are they trying to blind you with the meanings of words? Are they quickly going through verses so you would not notice any problems? All of these happen when they deal with doctrines.

We can see whether they are right or wrong. Why are they right or wrong? Many Christians point out a wrong prophecy that was never used in a gospel or the New

Testament. There is also a problem in the gospel and Paul's letter. A few scriptures or prophecies applied to someone besides Jesus.

Some people may get the wrong idea. I am not trying to deceive anyone. Look up the word "deceive" in the dictionary. I am not deceiving you. I want you to receive the Holy Spirit. I want you to have a very basic and good understanding of the Bible. Do I have the right to point out mistakes? Yes, I do.

What is deceive? Someone asking you to believe their lies or wrong ideas deceives you. They want you to believe their lies. The person who points out mistakes or brings out lies is not deceiving you. Actually, it is opposite of deceiving.

Let's say you're going to court—and you're innocent. You go to court with evidence, and your opponent comes with false evidence. You point out to the judge that he has the wrong evidence and ask him check it. If the judge is wise, he will check it and find out. A wise judge knows how reliable your opponent is. If you have a lazy judge who ignores the evidence that you present to him, would you be happy with him? Most people who commit crimes try to prove their innocence like a newborn. They try to change the evidence and make the judge believe you have committed the crime.

You are going to be the judge of this case. Please don't be a lazy judge. Please be a wise judge. Someone has committed a crime against God. They sowed tare in the field of God. Hebrews was written in AD 50-55. Psalm 110 contains the prophecy of King David. No other book discusses Psalm 110 completely. The other books discuss sections incompletely.

Does Christianity care? Does it understand why this is important? Hebrews made a huge mistake and was unbelievably twisted to deceive people using scripture in the wrong way. Hebrews speaks out in Psalm 110 to explain the right thing, but the early sections speak about Psalm 102, which was wrongfully added to prove Jesus is the Son of God, and he created heaven and earth.

> He has broken my strength in midcourse; He has shortened my days. "O my God," I say (King David), do not take me way in the midpoint of my life; you whose years endure throughout all generations. Long ago you laid the foundation of the earth: and the heavens are the work of your hands. They will perish, but you endure: they will all wear out like garment; You change them like clothing, and they pass away; but you are the same, and years have no end The children of your servants shall live secure; their offspring shall be established in your presence. (Ps. 102:23-28)

> But of the Son he (God) says, "And in the beginning, Lord, you founded the earth, and the heavens are the work of your hands; they will perish, but you remain; they will all wear out like clothing; like a cloak you will roll them

up, and like clothing they will be changed. But you are the same, and your years will never end." But to which of angels has he (God) ever said. (Heb. 1:8-13)

Do you see the problem? King David says God created heaven and earth. In Hebrews, God says Jesus has created earth and heaven. It is wrong and deceiving someone badly to prove Jesus is Son of God—and, in a sense, God the Son. They try to prove Jesus exists, but the author attempts to deceive. There is no reference or scripture where God says to anyone they created heaven and earth.

Another mistake this author made is: "therefore God, beyond you companions" (Heb. 1:9). Jesus has companions and anointed beyond all of them. "Among" means from many Jesus was anointed and among his companions means what? What does that mean to you? Who is he comparing Jesus with?

If Christian doctrine is stuck with New Testament for their beliefs, Jesus cannot be anything according to scripture. They point out prophecy or scriptures based on the New Testament. Don't we have the right check out if it really is in the Old Testament—and if the prophecy really applies? Do we only have the right to remain silent? The prophecies wrongly point this out in the New Testament. No one has original copies of the gospels or letters of the Bible. Someone may have added things. Even if it is the original copy, don't we have the right to know if the scriptures are used correctly? If they are wrong, you were deceived by someone using the wrong scripture to make false statements.

Understanding Psalm 110 holds the key to early Christianity. Why is this important to Christian doctrine?

> Stephen was filled with the Holy Spirit; he gazed into heaven and saw the glory of God and Jesus standing at right hand of God. "Look" he said, "I see the heavens opened and the Son of Man standing at the right hand of God!" (Acts 8:55-56)

> This Jesus God raised up. Being therefore exalted at right hand of God, King David himself says, "The Lord said to my Lord, 'sit at my right hand, until I make your enemies your footstool.' Therefore let the entire house of Israel know with certainty that God has made him both Lord and Messiah. (Acts 2:32-36)

> While Jesus was teaching in the temple, he said, "How can the scribes say that Messiah is the Son of David?" David himself, by the Holy Spirit declared; "The Lord said to my Lord, 'Sit at my right hand, until I put your enemies under your feet." David himself calls him Lord; so how can be his Son? (Mark 12:35-37)

Hebrews uses the complete section of Psalm 110. The first man killed for seeing Jesus at the right hand was Stephen in Acts 7. He had been killed for his vision of Jesus standing next to God. He also saw what side Jesus was at. It is important. Early Christianity started with Psalm 110.

> The Lord says to my Lord, "Sit at my right hand until I make your enemies your footstool The Lord sends out from Zion your mighty scepter. Rule in the midst of your foes. Your people will offer themselves willingly on the day you lead your forces on the holy mountains. For the womb of the morning, like dew, your youth will to you. The Lord has sworn and will not change his mind, "You are a priest forever according to the order of Melchizedek." The Lord is at your right hand; he will shatter kings on the day of his wrath. He will execute judgment among the nations, filling them with corpses; he will shatter heads over the wide earth. He will drink from the stream by the path; therefore he will lift up his head. (Ps. 110:1-7)

There are a lot of words that need to be understood in Psalm 110. Jesus was "exalted" to the right hand of God after he resurrected. What does "exalted" mean? Someone given higher power than before. Jesus's new position is at the right hand of God. He was never in the right hand before. "Until I make your enemies." As soon as Jesus's enemies become his slaves, God will send him down to the earth. "Until" means for a certain time period. After he was raised from death, God exalted at the right hand. He is not going to stay in that position forever. Who exalted Jesus? Is it God? Jesus did not exalt himself to the right hand of God. He was exalted because of his obedience to God.

"You are a priest forever according to the order of Melchizedek" (Ps. 110). There were a lot of arguments about Melchizedek on a website. Nobody argued about what a priest means or "what is priest for forever" means. This also applied to the man who is going to be at the right hand of the Father. What is a priest? A lot of you may have no idea and cannot picture what a priest is. I will give you better picture.

Have you ever seen an idol worshiper? Hindus worship idols. They have rules for priesthood. The temple priests do not do funerals. What do temple priests do? What is the relationship between idols? When a regular Hindu goes to a temple with his gift to God, that person does not offer a sacrifice to the idol and is not allowed to enter the idol's room; only a qualified person is allowed. That only person to enter God's room (God's hall) is a priest. The Hindu gives the gift to the priest.

The priest offers a sacrifice to the idol. Jews have a similar priesthood, but they do not offer gifts to idols. You could watch a YouTube video about Hindus and Jews. Jews offered cows, lambs, and doves as sacrifices to God. A person who offers a sacrifice to God is priest. He is not God. I heard Hindus saying they gave a gift to God. They never gave to God. They gave to a priest and the priest offered it to God. Jesus is a high priest who stands between you and God. He cannot be God if he is a priest of God. The priesthood given to Jesus is forever. He stands between man and God forever.

The priest and God are not equal. (Who is he a priest for?) However, most of the time, people say things in short form and assume the other person fully understands. For example, you may have heard Jesus died for your sins. This is not right. He died for the forgiveness of sin. There is a word missing. Both them are not the same. Each has a different meaning. However, when they say he died for your sins, they mean he died for the forgiveness of your sins. Some Christians argue that Stephen gave his soul or spirit to Jesus. They draw a conclusion and say Jesus is God. That is why Stephen and very early Christians gave their spirits and souls to Jesus. Their conclusion is wrong, according to Stephen. He saw a vision of Jesus at the right hand of God.

Early Christians knew Psalm 110 in detail—unlike today's Christians. They knew what a high priest means. They were very clear Jesus was a middleman. They knew who to offer their spirit or soul to as a sacrifice. They knew why. Many preachers have no idea what kind of priest the author of Hebrews was talking about? Without understanding the priesthood, preachers draw the wrong conclusion. I hope you understand why Stephen offered his spirit or soul to Jesus. He is the priest standing behalf of mankind.

The author in Hebrews compared it to Moses's priesthood. Why was Jesus the best priest? The author misused the word "forever." The priesthood was given to Jesus after he was exalted forever. The priesthood is forever. Somehow the author said Melchizedek is forever. The Old Testament never said that Melchizedek is forever. Jesus will be a priest forever, but Melchizedek will not.

Some Christian groups argue Jesus is Melchizedek based on some Gnostic writing. No. In Psalms 110, there must be a priesthood to worship God before Moses's priesthood. "Order of" becomes important. The priesthood that Melchizedek followed has existed forever. Somehow the author of Hebrews misunderstood or twisted the saying. The "Order of Melchizedek" means priests and kings. Jesus is the priest and king forever, according to Psalm 110.

The original author was an early Christian who tried to show the completeness of Psalm 110 to Jewish Christians, but someone rewrote Hebrews and introduced a different Jesus. It is wrong.

Jesus sits at the right hand of God. Is sitting beside the king an honor or a curse? "Sit at my right," God asks Jesus. What does that mean? I came from third world country. In third world countries, they beat their kids if their kids do something stupid as punishment. However, in North American countries, they don't beat their kids. If a kid does something stupid, they make the kid sit in the corner. It is like a punishment. Where you sit can be a curse or an honor.

The Queen of England celebrated her sixtieth anniversary on the throne. Who did she invite to her party? Who did she invite to her banquet? Sitting close to the queen is an honor. Who did she invite? At her dinner, who was sitting beside her? Her husband was on one side. Presidents, prime ministers, and kings sat on the other side. To sit beside her, you have to be a ruler. A ruler who committed a crime won't be invited.

At a certain age, boys want to be close to girls. This may not be possible unless she likes you. If a girl likes a guy, she wants him to ask her to be with him. I don't think girls ask. It is an unwritten rule or law. Sitting beside people is a request to be with them.

God ask Jesus to sit beside him at the right hand side. The request is an affection of love. God called Jesus to sit at the right hand. He anointed with him oil of gladness. That is how much God loved Jesus. He gave him authority and said, "You are my Son. I will be your Father and you will be my Son. Today I have begotten you."

God has authority over everything. God loved Jesus and gave him a new title and the authority to sit beside him with gladness and love. Jesus gained the love of God.

Who sees Jesus at the right hand of God? Only two individuals had a vision of Jesus at the right hand side of God. King David and Stephen saw it while they were filled with the Holy Spirit. Even though the apostles pointed out Jesus at the right side of God, they never saw it or mentioned it. The apostles watched as he was taken into the sky. The apostles claimed their witness for Jesus's resurrection.

Stephen's vision after the resurrection was an actual event, but King David's vision was a prophetic vision. Why was King David's vision prophetic? King David said, "Sit at my right hand, until I put your enemies under your feet" (Ps. 110).

If he had left God's right hand, come to earth, and emptied himself, he would be leaving God's right hand. Unless it was a prophetic vision, the prophecy has no meaning. We also know prophets see visions and hear voices. There are differences between a mentally ill person hearing voices or seeing visions and prophets seeing visions and hearing voices. Prophets are more like psychics. They know your past, what you do, and what you are going to do. A vision can be for a country or a small group of people.

We all know King David is a prophet. At his time, there were a lot of other prophets. The Bible doesn't have a title book for King David—even though he was one of the most talked about individuals in the Bible. His story is in another prophet's book. Samuel anointed two kings. When Saul was no good, he anointed King David. But in King David's time, prophets were called differently. Formerly in Israel, anyone who went to inquire of God, would say, "Come let us go to the seer"; for the one who is now called a prophet was formerly called a seer" (1 Sam. 9:9). Seers had prophetic visions. King David had futuristic prophetic visions. King David saw Jesus at the right hand only as an future event. Jesus was not at the hand right hand at the time. Jesus was at God's right hand after his resurrection. When David had the vision, Jesus was not in heaven or on earth.

Jesus at God's right hand was a big problem for Trinitarians. Trinitarians claim the invisible God is visible in the form of Jesus. According to King David and Stephen, God has a form by himself. The invisible God is capable of taking a visible form. That is what is clearly understandable from it.

Jesus is not a visible form of God. Since Jesus was called to sit down beside God, Jesus as the invisible form of God did not apply. Since Jesus sits at the right hand of God, he is not attacked as God's right hand.

CHAPTER 8

THE HISTORY OF JESUS

I repeat, If anyone proclaims to you a gospel contrary
to what you received, let that one be accursed!
—Galatians 1:9

I will explain the doctrine Jehovah's Witnesses, Pentecostals, and Catholics follow, what scriptures they follow to fit their doctrines, what words they were ignoring, and what is wrong with the scriptures they were using. That is going to be in the next chapters.

They won't completely explain Christian history. They will not explain history that leads to Jesus as the Son of God. It is very important to understand the Christian history if you want to follow very early Christianity. If you don't want to follow early Christianity, don't bother to read it. Get the Holy Spirit on the certificate. Keep believing in that you are supposed to get on certifacte as Christians. There are people who get angry if there are questions about their doctrines. They may not have answers, but they would curse even though Jesus told them not to curse anyone and bless the ones that curse you. Without understanding Christian history, there is no way to understand why we are in this mess. Christian history is available all over the Internet. Because this is not history book, I will only point out the history related to this topic.

There is a section of Christian history you need to understand in order to clearly understand why Jesus as God is a pagan idea. According to mainstream Christians—except Jehovah's Witnesses—Jesus was God. God and a god are different.

Let's look at Christian history when Jesus became God. In Christian history, Christianity grew up in an idol-worshipping pagan world. There was idol-worshipping religion in the Roman kingdom called paganism. Paganism was the official Roman religion. Some of the pagans converted to Christianity. They tried to preach to other pagans and Christians. Most pagans converted because they wanted to marry Christian women—not because of Christian preaching. Sexual love or the desire for beauty made them convert to Christianity.

Tertullian (AD 160-220) was an educated, bilingual man who married a Christian woman. He became a Christian through marriage. He became a priest for traditional Christians. He introduced two words to Christianity. One of them is the Trinity. The Trinity is different than how it was original introduced. The other idea he introduced was Jesus as one substance with God. He used the word *homoousios* from Greek pagan theology. His ideas were never approved by the early church fathers.

The idea of Jesus as "one substance" with God was rejected and it was asked not used it by church fathers in 264 at Antioch. Jesus as one substance with God was rejected by church fathers for a reason. Don't assume they just rejected it. Church fathers pointed out that "one substance" came from the idol-worshipping Greek pagan religion. It was pagan theology.

Pagans worshipped idols. Idol worship was understood by all as coming from the devil. Church fathers understood Greek pagans and other pagans were tied with the devil. That is what happened with Tertullian. That is the reason Tertullian's new doctrine was banned. He was a pagan introducing a pagan idea because he had just converted to Christianity. According to the Bible, people worship the idol-worshipping devil. Since it was from a devil religion, it is devilish. In other words, Jesus as one substance with God is coming from the devil. That is why the church fathers banned the use of the word Tertullian introduced. It is heretical according to the church fathers who are Catholic saints. Many main ideas used by today's church originated with Tertullian. He is not a saint. Tertullian quit traditional Christianity after less than ten years of service and joined another Christian sect called "montanists." Traditional Christians (today's Catholics) opposed it and called "montanists" heretical. Two things need to be noticed: church fathers rejected Tertullian's ideas—and Tertullian joined the heretics. However, his ideas are used by today's mainstream churches.

Heretical beliefs are not approved by the church. He never followed one religion or one sect of Christianity. He was not with traditional Christianity for long. He was a pagan in the first part of his life. He was with traditional Christians for ten years—and heretical (according to Catholics) until the end of his life

It is a shame no one uses Jesus's relationship to the Father based on the Bible. It has to borrow from a devilish religion to explain Jesus's relationship with God. The Bible did not have any scripture? Here is proof it was banned:

> The Synods of Antioch condemned the word *homoousios* (same substances) because it originated from pagan Greek. Synods of Antioch took place in 264 and 269 (http:en.wikipedia.org/wiki/ousios). Google "Tertullian" to find a source you like. Everyone knows he introduced the Trinity. Jesus is one substance with God.

How did a banned idea and word become the main faith of Christianity? In AD 325, Constantine decided to make Christianity an official religion. He set up a meeting. Traditional Christians joined that meeting and produced the Nicene Creed with the Roman king. They accepted that Jesus is one substance with God. Some Christians opposed it. The Nicene Creed writers had reasons for it.

A Christian sect emerged after a very big Roman war. It had a different doctrine than traditional Christians had. New groups started preaching some doctrines about Jesus. The Nicene Creed writers said they needed to reintroduce the one substance doctrine. The Nicene Creed says it is not possible to oppose them without reintroducing one substance. Who were the early church fathers? In AD 264? In AD 325? Which one is early Christianity? How come the Nicene Creed writers decided to use a word banned by their own church fathers? Why was it not important for them to convince the other side? How came they did not meet with the other side and discussed the matter since both were Christians? Why did the Nicene Creed fathers treat them as enemies? Why did they want the other side to be silenced? After the Nicene Creed came in to effect, no one was allowed to preach anything on Christianity except the Christian group that was in meeting with Constantine. Before AD 325, Jesus was not one substance with God.

This is how the pagan's devilish word "one substance" became an official and useable word in Christianity. Now it is the main doctrine of most denominations, but it was introduced by a pagan and is from a pagan religion. Why did it come from a pagan religion? Why didn't it bother the Nicene Creed fathers to use unscriptural words? Why didn't it bother them to use pagan words to describe Jesus? Pagans didn't care—only Christians cared about its origin.

Maybe I am repeating myself. I want you to have a clear understanding and make sure you understand it right. One substance is banned and announced as heretical in 264. In 325, it is reused—but it is not heretical. The Nicene Creed writers and today's church fathers want you to believe in heresy simply by telling you it is not heretical. It was heretical. It is not heretical anymore. Do you believe them because they say so? Why was it heretical in the first place? What God says is not important anymore, but what church fathers say about God using pagan theology is important to everyone. God is not mute. That is why God speaks through prophets. Also that is what God mentioned through the prophet.

When did the Trinity become the official theology of the Catholic Church? I am sure Macedonius played a villain for Catholics. Catholics brought the new Holy Spirit theory because of him. Because of him, Catholics decided to officially announce the Holy Spirit needed to be worshipped.

In 380, Tertullian was a hero, but Catholics rejected him as a church father and saint because he was not with them. Tertullian and Macedonius—and their surrounding Christian history—need to be understood in order to see what happened. Why do we believe so much wrong Christian theory, theology, and doctrine? We have said many blasphemies against God without realize Christian history and wickedness of political minded church fathers. Many are still thinking like slaves—not as children of God. Many still fear society and the church fathers. They won't question them. Even if they do, the priest or pastor won't have enough knowledge to give them the answer.

If there is no Tertullian Jesus is not the same substance as God. Is Jesus God? There are also problems with whether Jesus was a god or God. There is a difference between Jesus is God and Jesus is a God. Jesus is God means the same as substance with God. What is the difference between both questions? If Jesus is God, it leads toward the Trinity. That means Jesus is (not) God as himself with Father. The Trinity is God. They are joined with each other. But they are (not) separately God. It is not easy to describe. You cannot put are at same time you cannot put are not same time in one sentence. This is how the Trinity is nonsense. Cannot say are or are not. Cannot say is or is not. Tertullian ideas lead you to the Trinity and paganism. Jesus is a god leads toward the Bible prophecy, prophets, and scriptures.

Jehovah's Witnesses believe Jesus is a God. It is a difference I am going to point out. Jehovah's Witnesses believe he created heaven and earth after he was created by the Father. Usually Trinitarians and Jehovah's Witnesses argue about the same verses.

> He was image of the invisible God, Firstborn of all creation. For by him all things were created, both in the heavens and on earth, visible and invisible. (Col. 2:15-16)

Trinitarians say, "All things were created by him (Jesus)." Trinitarians argue that all means all. All means all for Trinitarians, but the Bible says differently. All does not mean all according the Bible.

> For God has put all the things in subjection under his feet. But when it says "all things are put in subjection, It is plain that this does not include the one who put all things are subjection under him. When all things are subjected to him, then the Son himself will also be subjected to the one who put all things in subjection under him, so that God maybe all in all. (1 Cor. 15:27-28)

Jehovah's Witnesses may claim history is on time in the Nicene Creed. They may point to the Arian side of history to prove some of their doctrines that related to Jesus as the first creation of God. Arian was a Christian sect that emerged in 318 after Constantine gave freedom of faith and took away freedom after signing the Nicene Creed.

How did Arian come to exist? In AD 300, the Roman king wanted to worship the sun god and follow paganism. At that time, some Christians were hidden. Some changed religions because of the fear of been killed. After Constantine took over, Romans were allowed to practice their own religions. Christians opened up colleges in Antioch, Rome, and Alexandria, Egypt. Arius, an Alexandrian priest, announced Jesus was the first creation of God. Priests around him joined him. The Alexandrian bishop got jealous. He kicked Arius out of the church.

The church fathers were teaching Jesus was the Son of God. He exists and is joined with God. Arius never argued against the begotten Son. Arian Christians and traditional Christians argued about the time of Jesus's existence.

Arius claimed, "God was not Father all the time. There was a time God just lived as God." What does this mean? For example, if you are married, you are husband or wife for a while. When you get a child, you are a father or a mother. Unless you have a child, you are not the father or mother. There was period you were not a father or mother—just someone's spouse. If you are a father or mother when you have a child, Arius's argument makes sense. Do not forget Jesus is not God's wife or twin brother or brother. That is why Arius's argument makes sense.

God was the Father to no one for a while. He only became a Father when he begotten someone or he created someone. Do you see why Aryanism grew up? Christian sects had similar beliefs to Arians—even though they did not join with Arius.

However, Arian and Aryanism grew wildly. His beliefs were scriptural and from the Bible. The problem is some scriptures were falsely written even before Aris. I am questioning some of those scriptures. In the Bible, God never said anyone corrupted the scripture. In fact, God warned us about false statements in the Bible (Jer. 8:8). Paul warned there were unacceptable gospels circulating.

The Bible never asks you to believe 100 percent. Are you going to take God's word? Or are you going to believe some doctrine that tells you to believe 100 percent? History goes far beyond AD 300. There is one more problem—the Nicene Creed fathers added a book to the Bible with respect to Constantine.

Jesus is God and a god only if you don't know the history and don't carefully read the Bible.

CHAPTER 9

BRAND-NEW JESUS

For if someone comes and proclaims another Jesus than the one we
proclaimed, or if you receive a different spirit from the one you received, or
a different gospel from the one you accepted,
you submit to it readily enough.
—2 Corinthians 11:4-5

In the twentieth century, Western countries were producing new cars. There were new models, new manufacturers, and different prices. Many of them still produce a lot of cars today.

Somehow in the first century until the end of the fourth century, the Christian community was producing different Jesuses. Some Christians even rewrote Paul's letter and the gospels. Since there are no original copies, we have to rely on the Old Testament's prophecy. Whoever tried to produce new Jesuses misused a lot of prophecies. I already showed you how the author of Hebrews twisted King David's prayer in Psalm 102 to fit his theory. It is solid proof that the Christian community was trying deceive others by using unfit Bible verses.

However, books or sections of books that were used to deceive still exist in the New Testament. Jehovah's Witnesses and Trinitarians have different beliefs about Jesus—sometimes based on the same chapters of the same book. Even though I understand it is corrupt and unfit, I will write down so you know where the scriptures are and what scriptures are used by these sects.

Which of Jesus's disciples proclaimed? Trinitarians are using scriptures from the Bible that they claim are from Paul. The problem is no one has the original copies. It has been rewritten many times. Since that was the case, they claim it fit for Jesus. Otherwise, it is deceiving. People are already deceived. Do not think I am going to deceive with my writings. My writing will prove you have been deceived. I already mentioned Jehovah's Witnesses are not Trinitarians. They believe Jesus is very first creation of God. Other evangelicals and Catholics believe Jesus is God himself—but a separate person. I will

41

show you what scripture they use and the problem with the scripture and words they ignored.

Who was Jesus before coming to world? This scripture is pointed at by theologians from Jehovah's Witnesses and Trinitarians.

> Who, though he was in the form of God, did not regard equality with God as something to be exploited, But emptied himself, taking the form of a slave, being born in human likeness. And begin found in human form, He humbled himself and become obedient to the point of death—even death on a cross. Therefore God also highly exalted him and gave him the name that is above every name, so that at the name of Jesus every knee should bend, in heaven and on earth and under the earth, and every tongue should confess that Jesus Christ is the Lord, to the glory of God. (Phil. 2:6-11)

Trinitarians use this verse and to show Jesus is God and comes from heaven. However, Philippians doesn't point out any prophecy. This song has a problem "in the form of God." Why is there "form" in the middle of the sentence? Why didn't they write: "Did God come down form of Jesus" there? That would make the Trinitarian claims right.

What was in the form of God mean? Does that mean angels? The author in Hebrews says, "You have made them for a little lower than angel. Yet you have made them a little lower than God" (Ps. 8:5). Their belief was based on Bible verse. That is why I point this out to you.

King David's saying is not exactly the same as Hebrews 2:7. If the song in Philippians said, "Didn't God came down in the form of Jesus," it would make sense. Or God took a form of man in name of Jesus would make sense. Since neither was said, I don't think they came from early Christianity. There is no scriptural proof from the Old Testament.

There is another problem with "God exalted Him." If he is joined with God, no one needs to exalt God. That is a higher position than anything and anybody. Jesus was exalted by God.

According to Philippians, God wanted Jesus to be honored only after God has exalted him when he renders into heaven. If he exists with God, everything is already under his foot and no one needs give him authority of anything. And we don't need to wait for his return because we believe his enemy at his footstool is not going to return. If he left God's hand right hand in order to come to earth, the prophecy might have been fulfilled already. The word exalted after his resurrection would have no meaning like Peter proclaimed in Acts 2.

Why does a person have a name? A name is used to identify a person. Everyone knows Charlie Chaplin. A person gets famous based on his actions. Charlie Chaplin is a comedian. He was famous for his actions. His name doesn't identify his actions.

Jesus is not the right name. Jesus's name is Yeashu. There were thousands of Yeashus in Jesus's time. Jesus is known for not his name but for his actions. A person's name identifies his character, authority, and abilities. For example, kings or queens are honored by their citizens and the law system.

Why would a regular a person's name be honored by the law system? Kings are honored for their position and their intelligence. In June 2012, the Queen of England was honored for sixty years of ruling. A lot of other rulers went to London and congratulated her. Was she honored for her name? Was she honored because of who she is? I know at least two ladies who have the same name—those two never got to rule anything).

Why does Jesus's name need to be honored? God gave him authority. We can just honor any Jesus. There was a murderer named Jesus. Do we honor him? We need a name to identify someone's ability, authority, and character so we can quickly understand that identity. What name a person has may not be important, but the abilities, authorities, and character are important.

Angels appear to be translated as God. Being equal with God and joined with God are different things. According to the Trinity, Jesus existed with God. If they exist and joined Jesus was exalted after entering heaven. When was the Holy Spirit going to be exacted by God? Why should we mind a song that has no proof from the Old Testament? How do we accept Jesus came to earth according to prophecy if there was no prophecy given? Why should we accept it? Is Jesus the visible form of God?

> He (God) has rescued us from the power of darkness and transferred us into the kingdom of his beloved Son, in whom we have redemption, the forgiveness of sins. He is the image of the invisible God, the firstborn of all creation; for in him all thing in heaven and on the earth were created, things visible and invisible, whether thorns or dominions or rulers or powers—all things have been created through him and for him. He is the head of the body, the church; he is the beginning, the firstborn from the dead, so that he might come to have first place in everything. For in him all the fullness of God was pleased to dwell, and though him God was pleased to reconcile to himself all things, whether on earth or in heaven, by making peace through the blood of cross. (Col. 1:13-20)

No scripture from Old Testament pointed it out. It is unknown. It is unknown which prophecy the author was basing it on. "All things in heaven and on the earth were created through him." Please don't conclude the author was telling heaven and earth was created by Jesus. The author was using the words "in heaven." It was different when he created heaven. The author said "in"—that means already created. Who created heaven and earth?

Invisible God and first creation of God are debated by Jehovah's Witnesses, Trinitarians, and other the individuals. However, Trinitarians argue, "All means all." Trinitarians say what is exactly in the scripture. So far, no one argued against it. I came across a verse while I was reviewing the resurrection. It was plain that all does not include God; Jesus is under God's authority (1 Cor. 15:27). Everything or all things are under Jesus's authority. It does not say all things under him because his image is of God. It was plain that it does not include God if his image of God has no meaning. Now, it is clearly understandable that all does not mean all according Bible verse. And his is not a form of the invisible God.

Is Jesus begotten son or first begotten son or only begotten son of God? Trinitarians claim Jesus is the only begotten Son. Who are the second and third children of all creation? Does God have other begotten sons? "First born of all creation" Colossian 1:15. Born means begotten Son. There was an argument that Jesus was born—not created.

The highlighted word is firstborn. Some Bibles removed "only begotten" from the Gospel of John. "First begotten" may describe the love and attention a parent gives to their first child. The first child may not be the parents' favorite, but they give it more attention and respect. All parents respect older children.

Some early Christians believe Jesus is an angel. Someone tried to hide that belief by changing writing. I do not think those songs were from original writings. Someone might have added those songs. I do not think Jesus is an angel or God. These are brand-new versions of Jesus from early Christianity, which Pauline Christian intruders were probably spreading.

Trinitarians show Jesus is a better than angel and begotten Son, according to scripture. Earlier I discussed how the prophecy has been twisted. However, let's look at the claim and see the words they ignore.

God said, "You are my Son; today I have begotten you." "I will be his Father, and he will be my Son." When God brings the firstborn into the world, he says, "Let all God's angels worship him." Of the angel, he says, "He makes his angel's wings, and his servants flames of fire."

> Your throne, O God, is forever and ever, and the righteous scepter is the scepter of your kingdom. You have loved righteous and hated wickedness; therefore God, your God, has anointed you with the oil of gladness beyond your companions. Andin the beginning, Lord, you found the earth, and the heaven are work of your hands; they will perish, but remain; they will all wear out like clothing; like a cloak you will roll them up, and like clothing they will be changed. But you are the same and your years will never end. Sit at my right hand until I make your enemies a footstool for your feet. (Heb. 1:5-13)

Someone is trying to tell Hebrews or Jewish Christians who already believe Jesus is an angel. It seems some early Christians believed Jesus is an angel. The author of Hebrews is unknown. However, Pauline Christians had copies. That is why it is commonly known as one of Paul's book.

"Look, God says you are my Son." This is what Trinitarians try to show you. The main problem is Hebrews has been twisted. (I will ignore it for now.) I want you to see what tense is used. "You "will be" my Son." Jesus will be God's Son in the future. He was not his Son when this prophecy was proclaimed in the Old Testament. Why are tenses important? There was a debate between Jesus and the Sadducees about the Resurrection. Did Jesus tell them to check the tense on scripture? Whether it is applied to Jesus or not is another matter. The author of Hebrews introduced a brand-new Jesus.

"You are my Son and today begotten" are present. And some copycat preachers argue from coding one of church fathers said that present is always present. Jesus was always God the Son. Here is the problem: according to the same book, today does not mean today in prophecy. The author of Hebrews simply points out why today is a future event in prophecy. Who do we trust—early church fathers or logical scripture from the Bible? Again he sets a certain day through David.

"Today, if you hear his voice, do not harden your hearts. For if Joshua had given them rest, God would not speak later about another day" (Heb. 4:7-8). This matters because there was theology about Jesus's existence as the Son of God. The Son of God has no beginning and no ending.

Jehovah's Witnesses believe he existed a very long time ago. How long? Even before the universe existed. "Will be my Son" is not past tense or present tense.

This didn't add up. Trinitarians claim, "Anointed you with the oil of gladness beyond your companions." What are companions? There is also a reason applied for the special anointment. Who were Jesus's companions? Trinitarians simply don't care what tense is applied. Jesus said the blind cannot lead the blind. The priests were leading the people. Always we focused on leaders, but the blind people who were following them were out of focus. These three songs are used by mainstream churches to fit their doctrines. They never used in full; they already know it contradicts their theology and doctrine.

According to Paul, there are different Jesuses. Perhaps, Paul didn't like the new Jesuses. He loved his old Jesus. He worried they had already fooled and accepted the brand-new Jesus. According to Paul, the new Jesuses were wrong. Who accepted the new Jesus? The Christians. It was not the pagans who accepted the new Jesus.

Paul seemed to be upset with Christians—not with Jews or pagans. There were a lot of new ideas floating around in early Christian communities.

> I am astonished that you are so quickly deserting the one who called you
> in the grace of Christ and are turning to a different gospel—not that there

is another gospel, but there are some who are confusing you and want to pervert the gospel of Christ. But even if we or an angel from heaven should proclaim to you a gospel contrary to what we proclaimed to you, let that one be accursed! As we have said before, so now I repeat, if anyone proclaims to you a gospel contrary to what you received, let that one be accursed! (Gal. 1:6-9)

For if someone comes and proclaims another Jesus than the one we proclaimed, or if you receive a different spirit from the one you received, or a different gospel from the one you accepted, you submit to it readily enough. (2 Cor. 11:4-5)

This indicated there was other gospels existed besides Paul's. Was it in writing? It was very clear Pauline Christians had those copies with them and that's why Paul asked to reject it. Why did they accept the new model of Jesus? Paul didn't indicate that in his letters. We are not certain if they ignored Paul and accepted another Jesus.

When a group of people has different ideas, someone may strongly believe the other side. It is unclear if Paul won over the Galatians with his letter. Maybe they got his letter and ignored him. I was wondering if the bishops received the letter. What happened if he changed the words in the letter and reproduced it to a regular audience? The letters might have been received by one individual but not read in public.

If Paul was the original author of Galatians and Timothy, he was producing two different versions of Jesus. Paul warned of Jewish spies among the Christians. They were capable of changing the writing. Galatians accepted the new Jesus—not Timothy. Christ means Messiah.

What was Paul proclaiming? Which was the gospel? Can he proclaim two different Jesuses—one for Galatians and another for Timothy?

Remember Jesus Christ, raised from the dead, a descendant of David. That is my gospel for which I suffer hardship, even to the point being chained like a criminal (2 Tim. 2:8-9)

Trinitarians and Jehovah's Witnesses claim Jesus descended only through the Virgin Mary. "God had sent his Son, born of a woman, born under the law" (Gal. 4:4). There would be problem in theology if Jesus is from a virgin. This is not from the apostles. It was after the time of the apostles.

Most apostles claim that Jesus is the Son of David. "Born of woman" does not indicate a virgin birth. When it comes to birth, we are all born of woman. Galatians perhaps inserted it to produce a new Jesus.

We will discuss which Jesus is right and which Jesus Paul proclaimed in the next chapters. We are also going to look at some claims in the Old Testament prophecy regarding Jesus. We will look at the Apostles' Creed. Some preachers want you to believe in the Apostles' Creed. Even though all of these have been discussed with them, they don't have a clue the name and creed are fake. The Apostles' Creed does not belong to the apostles.

"For us there is one God, and one mediator between God men, the man Christ Jesus" (1 Tim. 2:4).

CHAPTER 10

WHY APOSTLES WORSHIPPED JESUS

Most verses preachers and theologians point out lead nowhere. They are only preaching for lazy Christians. Christians are careless because it is their religion. They have to marry someone in the church and follow other people to be social. They don't care. They aim to live around their societies. Their aim is not to get close to God.

Many people are like that. They protect their unknown faith and unknown beliefs. They don't even know why they believe certain things. If a strong question rises against their faith, they protest. Protest is not the answer.

Someone told me Christians protest like Middle Eastern religions; they would kill you if you write like these. When I met other people's challenges, I was insulted and threatened. Most of time, I broke their challenges. What I want you to do simply don't make challenges. If challenges are met, you need to be changed—not me.

Please don't panic; we are also human. Human faith has been changed during every age of the world. I changed my faith. Christianity changed from Jewish. Now it is very hard for many to believe in the original Christianity, which is no longer exists.

Is Jesus a god? Not as He is the creator of heaven and earth. As a prophet, he is God because God called his prophets gods. If the most high is calling someone God, that is a very strong statement. I would mind calling Jesus s God. Big boss called him boss. However, he is the big boss.

"You (Moses) shall serve as God for him (Aaron)" (Ex. 4:17). "I (God) say 'You are Gods, children of the most high, all of you'" (Ps. 82:6). Why are prophets called gods? They work for God. God honored them by calling them gods. Most theologians agree with it. However, they ask if the prophet was ever worshipped? They point out that Jesus was worshipped by his disciples.

Trinitarians claim Jews know better; they do not worship except God. Jesus's disciples were not regular Jews. They were better at understanding Jewish law and scripture because they were with Jesus. Therefore, he is God. Whoever has that idea is wrong. Probably they haven't read about Elisa. Yes, they were worshipped prophets.

When the company of prophets at Jericho saw him at a distance, they declared, "The spirit of Elijah rests on Elisa." They came to meet him and bowed to the ground before him" (2 Kings 2:15-16). Other prophets were worshipping a prophet. It is not someone who does not know God's law; they were prophets or followers of Elijah who worshipped another prophet. Prophets worshipped a man—not some regular Jewish man. Did they not know the law? A man had been worshipped. Other prophets may have been worshipped too.

Some preachers believe Isaiah wrote about Jesus even though none of the writing in the New Testament claimed it. They e-mail me and say, "Look. It is about Jesus." Many people have no idea that the prophecy is not only about Jesus. All prophecies, all time is not about Jesus. Isaiah's prophecy never applied to Jesus.

> For unto us a child is born, unto us a Son is given: and the government shall be upon his shoulder: and his name shall be called wonderful counselor, the mighty God, the everlasting Father, the prince of peace. Of the increase of is government and peace there shall be no end, upon the throne of David, and upon his kingdom, to establish it with justice from henceforth even forever. The zeal of the Lord of hosts will perform this. The Lord sent a word into Jacob, and it hath lighted upon Israel." (Isa. 9:6-8)

Who is Isaiah talking about what is he means "for us." We already discussed how Immanuel means God with us—"God with Judea"—and not with Israel. "But man of God came to him said, 'O king, do not let the army of Israel go with you, for the Lord is not with Israel—all these Ephraimites" (2 Chron. 25-7).

For Judea, a child is given as ruler. A child! What is a child? A child is not a young man. A government will be given to a child. That child needs to carry the responsibility of ruling Judea. "Unto us a Son is given" simply means it was not a female ruler. He would have four code names. This prophecy was already fulfilled fifty years after Isaiah's time.

Remember the story about a child king who was to become a ruler in house of David as God promised. There was a wicked female queen who was after Isaiah's time. Isaiah's "unto us a Son" becomes important. The Isaiah chapter 9:6-8 prophecy about this child king. This child king was holding a key to the prophecy's code name. For the next round of King David's son's kingship, he was a father. He is like a second father to all David's kings. All the next kings were from this child. He restored God's law in Israel.

This never applied to Jesus at all. Jesus was a man at thirty-three—raised from the dead. From that time, God appointed him as king (Lord). Not when he was child. That is why "Jesus was exalted" needs to be understood clearly. The government needed to be at child shoulder order for this prophecy full filled not at 33 years old man. Jesus was not a ruler when he was a child. When he returns to rule, he will be a man. This prophecy is still important to Jesus's genealogy.

"Remember that Jesus Christ of the seed of David was raised from dead according to gospel" (2 Tim. 2:7).

CHAPTER 11

SINLESS JESUS

Some Christians believe Jesus is a rejected messiah of the Jewish people. And they believe he is the Son of God who was sent to earth to redeem us from sin. Can the Son of God and Son of David be the same man?

In general, anyone who receives the Holy Spirit is a child of God. Mainstream Christianity claims Jesus is the begotten Son of God. God never made any promise he would send his Son to earth to redeem us from sin. Every prophecy in the Bible, such as the virgin birth, is applied to something else and some part of history a regular a person won't understand.

No one is capable of understanding every section of the history that is related to prophecies. People take advantage of it and twist the verse to fit their claims or theology—even while the apostles were living. The apostles never argued with the Jewish leaders about those prophecies of the virgin birth.

The stories of Matthew and Luke don't add up. According to Luke, Jesus was circumcised after eight days. Matthew claimed the wise men met Jesus in Bethlehem and Joseph ran to Egypt to save Jesus. Did Jesus go to Jerusalem for his circumcision?

The Son of God leads you toward the virgin birth. The Son of David leads you through the messiah. Both cannot be true. There were some arguments. A lot of preachers say Jesus's genealogy can be traced through Mary to make us believe the virgin birth was true. First of all, the virgin birth was never prophesized. God never promised to send his Son to save the earth.

The apostles were dying to prove Jesus was the messiah, according to the promise that God made to King David. The promise was the Son of David would rule the earth forever. The virgin birth was just pagan theology. Definitely, it was not God's prophecy.

> When they heard this, they were emerged and wanted to kill them. And every day in the temple and a home they did not cease to teach and proclaim Jesus as the Messiah. (Acts 5:33-42)

There are many other Christian theologies based on the virgin birth since mainstream Christians believe in the virgin birth. Catholics took it into a lot of theologies. And Christians believe in original sin. Catholics baptize infants based on original sin. Catholics theory was not based on scripture. It is called Immaculate Conception.

What is Immaculate Conception? Mary was sinless when she conceived Jesus—or after she conceived. However, original sin and the Immaculate Conception contradict each other.

What is original sin? Sin continues through generations—from the father to the son. Does it not apply to women? Do we baptize women? Can original sin not come from a mother? Can it? Do men carry sin in the family tree? Many Catholics believe Mary came from a virgin mother. She was also sinless. However, Catholics officially condemned it. However, concept doctrine and original sin theory have bound together. It confuses them.

Why is the Immaculate Conception important for original sin theory? Mary would be a sinner if she has a human father. Jesus's genealogy continues through Mary. Jesus would have sin in his blood. Therefore he could not be a sacrifice for human sin.

They are confused and claim Mary's mother was a virgin. There was no original sin in her blood. In order for Jesus to have no sin in his blood, his mother, grandmother, and great-grandmother had to be virgins.

Other Catholics have a better idea. Mary is special and without original sin because God granted special permission when she conceived Jesus. However, that is not the case. The virgin birth has many problems.

The Immaculate Conception was introduced in 1854. How do you understand virgin theory leading you against God's promise to King David? Don't think I hate Catholics or the Virgin Mary. I observe and question my beliefs. I believe I was asked to believe and follow. Like any churchgoing Catholic, I said prayers based on this theory. I heard a lot of songs and sang a few verses based on this doctrine.

A lot of people believe I don't have the freedom of speak. If I find problems, quit Catholicism and join someone else. What happens when a scientist's mouth is shut? The world would still be flat. Galileo was prisoned for speaking up and introducing his observations. He was successful and overcame the others. If he shut his mouth and feared for his life, the world won't be the same today. I write for the benefit of others. You have the right to find mistakes in my observations. All I am doing is observing my faith—or the faith I used to believe in.

Apollos powerfully refuted the Jews in public, showing the scripture that the Messiah is Jesus (Acts 18:28). There was no scripture before the New Testament. The virgin birth was never told in the Old Testament.

CHAPTER 12

FAKE NAME, FAKE CREED

For someone comes and proclaims another Jesus than one we proclaimed,
or if you receive a different the Holy Spirit from the one you received, or a
different gospel from the one you accepted,
you submit to it readily enough.
—2 Corinthians 11:4

Why should you not follow a fake creed? Where did the Apostles' Creed come from? Many Christian preachers believe the Apostles' Creed came from Jesus's first disciples. In fact, it is not.

The Apostles' Creed originated around AD 180 in an unknown group. Christians who lived in those days were not apostles. They were called church fathers. Some of them converted to Christianity to marry Christian women. In the fifth century, Catholics added few verses and named it the Apostles' Creed. They made it a prayer during Mass.

If you are Catholic, the prayer says, "I believe in one God." There are two versions of it. One is called the Apostles' Creed, and other is called the Nicene Creed. Since they named it the Apostles' Creed, everyone calls it the Apostles' Creed.

When I or someone else points out mistakes, they say we are preaching according to the Apostles' Creed. All of them assume it was from the apostles. They stupidly believe it without checking its origins. They have the wrong idea about where it originated. Paul warned about different doctrines, but he never advised anyone to follow the Apostles' Creed. Why? Because they don't have it. If the apostles had a creed, would Paul simply ask Corinthians and Galathian stick with it? Why he would be warning different Jesus gospel and Holy Spirit?

The Apostles' Creed has many mistakes. First of all, Jesus's first disciples and Paul were dying hard to prove Jesus was the Messiah.

Remember Jesus Christ, raised from the dead, a descendant of David—that is my gospel. For which I suffer hardship, even to the point of being chained like criminal. But the word of God is not chained." (Tim. 2:8)

Notice what Paul said. For Paul, there is no other gospel. Peter said descendants of King David raised and sat at the right hand of God. Descendants of King David completely ignored the Apostle's Creed. That was never included in the Apostles' Creed. The virgin birth was never preached by the first disciples.

If the Apostles' Creed originated with the apostles, would they make a line for it? The Apostles' Creed is asking people to believe in the Holy Spirit rather than receive the Holy Spirit. Believing the Holy Spirit is not a solid sentence. How to believe is not explained. And what to believe is not explained. The Apostles' Creed was named by Catholics. "I believe in the Catholic Church" was added in the fifth century. Pentecostal preachers were asking their followers to believe the Apostles' Creed. The Bible preaches about receiving the Holy Spirit.

For someone comes and proclaims another Jesus than one we proclaimed, or if you receive a different Holy Spirit from the one you received, or a different gospel from the one you accepted, you submit to it readily enough. (2 Cor. 11:4)

This clearly points out the apostles preached about receiving and made sure people accepted Jesus and received the Holy Spirit. On the other hand, the Apostles' Creed only wants you to believe in the Holy Spirit and says nothing about receiving the spirit. Can you see the difference?

In the Apostles' Creed, almost all sentences start with "I believe." That is the opposite of what the Bible says. The Apostles' Creed says, "I believe in one God." In the Bible, God says his Commandments. Believe is a fuzzy word.

Why was Paul advising this to Corinthians who had already received the Holy Spirit? God would tell Corinthians through the Holy Spirit what was right and wrong. God would tell them who was preaching them wrong.

Paul already preached about a different Jesus. That was why he was advising this to people who had already received the Holy Spirit. It was already happening in Paul's time. Even in Paul's time, unknown Jesuses or different Jesuses were proclaimed by someone. The Jesus Paul proclaimed is important if we care what Paul was warning about. We cannot ignore what was said in Paul's time.

What is happening today in Christianity is wrong. They applied this to today's churches. Ignore the fact it was said in Paul's time. People proclaimed different Jesuses might have been proclaiming to Corinthians. Paul wrote it to point out the different Jesuses and different gospels. Who was doing it? It might have been a Jewish group trying to destroy Christianity or a Christian group who proclaimed different ideas about Christianity. Did the Apostles' Creed proclaim a different Jesus and a different Holy Spirit? Yes! It did.

There were at least four creeds after AD 300. Most of them turned into Catholic prayers. Usually ideas do not support the Bible. A Bible reader would say the creeds are different than the Bible. Before every creed, there would be a meeting. A political leader would take the center chair. All the opponents were ignored because of the political situations at the time. Jesus was against religious leaders because they were wrong.

Jesus becomes the right path to God. Religious leaders lead their disciples in the opposite direction. They perform religious duties as the books and priests taught. Most churches believe you will go to hell if you do not follow the rules.

The Apostles' Creed says, "He will come again the judge of the livings and dead." Christianity held two beliefs about the dead: you would go to heaven or the resurrection. Which one are we supposed to believe? Whatever happens after death, we have to face it.

I visited an evangelical church. They thought they were following early Christianity. The preacher said, "I will build my church, and the gates of Hades will not prevail against it. I will give you the keys of the kingdom of heaven, and whatever you bind on earth will be found in heaven, and whatever you loose on earth will be loosed in heaven" (Matt. 16:18-19).

Did Jesus really say that? The church I visited had existed for less than thirty years. Peter lived two thousand years ago. No church has existed for two thousand years—especially not evangelical churches. Someone who does not know history might think about Catholic churches. The devil controlled the church for some time. They also were overcome by Napoleon. Therefore, it is not about them. Catholicism started around AD 400.

A Catholic woman married someone from another denomination. She decided to stay Catholic. She said, "It is singular not plural." She didn't realize the next verse said, "Hades will not prevail." She didn't know Catholic history. She assumed Catholicism had existed since Peter's time.

Peter did not have the key to heaven. In Revelation, Jesus has the key to heaven. What happens when Jesus return on second coming? Angels would be with him. They would gather the people of earth. There was no scripture where the apostles would be at the second coming.

Are the apostles going to be resurrected from the dead? I was wondering if Peter was resurrected already and went to heaven. Is he in heaven now? It is unclear since the second coming and the dead going to heaven contradict each other. Would Jesus's disciples be resurrected on the last day or at the second coming?

The idea of heaven and last days contradict each other. Jesus went to heaven after resurrection. Did Peter and others go to heaven without resurrection? The Apostles' Creed says, "He will come to judge living and the dead." Where would Peter would be?

Is he going to be in heaven already? If you believe in the second coming, Jesus wouldn't have said it.

I believe Jesus never said Matthew 16:18-19. Someone may have added that to support Peter. It only appears in Matthew.

Many people think they follow true Christianity. They think they are wearing pure Christianity, but they are spiritually poor and do not have enough knowledge or faith to find out if it is fake. They are paid little amounts of money and can only afford to buy fake gold.

People who sell or wear fake gold are not going to tell you the quality. Gold jewelers know how to check for pure gold. People cannot afford to buy pure gold jewelry; there is no point discussing pure gold jewelry with the poor. They are not going to buy it anyway. Many Christians want to buy pure gold (follow early Christianity). Is it possible? Many sell fake gold or gold mixed with cheap metal—and some people think it is real gold. When they test gold for quality, the fake gold would be visible. Some fake doctrines may look real, but you will not know until you test the quality. There is no benefit to carrying fake gold.

A lot of preachers might tell you to follow the Apostles' Creed. If you question their preaching, they will ignore you. Some people may insult you. It is better to ask God. God will help you with scriptures (Isa. 54:13). Be like Nova. God decides your life after death—and while you live.

"For from the least to the greatest of them, everyone is greedy for unjust gain; and from prophet to priest, everyone deals falsely" (Jer. 6:13).

CHAPTER 13

WHY TEN COMMANDMENTS?

Wrote for them the many things of my law,
but they regarded them as something alien.
—Hosea 8:12

What shall we say? Is the law sin? Certainly not! I would not have known what sin was except for the law. I would not have known what coveting really was if the law had not said "do not covet" (Rom. 7:7).

Why are there ten commandments? They explain what sin is. Who wrote the Ten Commandments? God wrote them.

God gave his commandments to Moses twice. Moses broke them the first time. God gave them to Moses a second time. The commandments did not belong to Moses. They belonged to God. It is important to clearly understand that God gave the commandments. They are God's commandments. Nobody has the authority to add or subtract—except God.

Anybody who disobeys God's commandments or hides God's commandments is adding and subtracting from the Word of God. I strongly believe that God knows what commandments to give—better than any religion, any group, or person. God is not stupid. Religion, you, and I can be stupid. God knows what commandments to give; if we are his people and want a relationship with God, we must obey them.

The Ten Commandments

1. You shall not have any other Gods before me (Ex: 20:3).
2. You shall not make graven image, bow down, or worship to it (Ex. 20:4-5).
3. You shall not misuse the name of the Lord your God (Ex: 20:7).
4. Remember the Sabbath day by keeping it holy (Ex: 20:8).
5. Honor your father and mother (Ex: 20:12).

6. You shall not murder (Ex: 20:13).
7. You shall not commit adultery (Ex: 20:14).
8. You shall not steal (Ex: 20:15).
9. You shall not bear false witness (Ex: 20:16).
10. You shall not covet your neighbor's house. You shall not covet your neighbor's wife, or his manservant, maidservant, his ox or donkey, or anything that belongs to your neighbor (Ex: 20:17).

I have problems with the religions that altered the Ten Commandments. As far as is I know, the Ten Commandments were written in two places: Exodus and Deuteronomy.

You shall not covet your neighbor's wife. You shall not set your desire on your neighbor's house or land, his manservant, maidservant his ox or donkey or anything that belong to your neighbor (Deut 5:21). Neighbor is the subject—not wife.

The Ten Commandments do not covet anything that belongs to your neighbor and make a list of it. In Exodus 20:17 and Deuteronomy 5:21, the subject is neighbor. They are not two commandments. It is one commandment. It has only one verse number in Exodus and Deuteronomy.

The Catholic Ten Commandments

1. You shall not have any other gods before me.
2. You shall not misuse the name of the Lord your God.
3. Remember the Sabbath day by keeping it holy.
4. Honor your father and mother.
5. You shall not murder.
6. You shall not commit adultery.
7. You shall not steal.
8. You shall not bear false witness.
9. You shall not covet your neighbor's wife.
10. You shall not covet your neighbor's goods.

They consider the long list from Exodus and Deuteronomy as one commandment. But it is not one commandment. It is two. That is why people learn to disagree and argue based on their verbal knowledge. They do not understand it needs to be followed with respect to God. No one serves the master. Is God is your master?

They teach and learn nine commandments only. They have to divide the tenth commandment into two pieces. This is how religion is fooling people. (I have learned that ten from that religion, whenever I went to as question they try to fool, telling to read a book with thousands of pages yet they are not reading a half of pages of Deuteronomy, tell me to their website.)

Here is what I found out about the Ten Commandments from the official Roman Catholic book (catechism). Here are two paragraphs from Catholic catechism that talk about history of the Commandments

Ever since St. Augustine, the Ten Commandments have occupied a prominent place in the catechisms of baptismal candidates and faithful. In the fifteenth century, the custom arose of expressing the commandments of the Decalogue in a rhymed formula, easy to memorize, and in positive forms. They are still in use today. The catechism of the church has often expounded on Christian morality by following the order of the Ten Commandments.(Catechism, ten comm section two verse 2065-not bible verse)

The division and numbering of the commandments have varied the course of history. The present catechism follows the division of the commandments established by St. Augustine, which have become traditional in the Catholic Church. It is also of the same in the Lutheran Confessions. The Greek fathers worked out a slightly different division, which is found in the Orthodox Church and reformed communities.(Catechism, ten comm, section two verse 2066-not bible verse)

- They are St. Augustine's Ten Commandments—not God's.
- Rhyme and easy to memorize for whom? (What language?)
- Division and number by St. Augustine
- Did not have any theologian in the Catholic community to put Ten Commandments in the right order for almost sixteen centuries
- Isn't important to know the commandments?
- Who is St. Augustine?

Here is the problem. He had a pagan father and a Christian mother. He was baptized at thirty-two in AD 386 after he met St. Ambrose. St. Ambrose was baptized at age forty in AD 370. St. Ambrose and St. Augustine both did not have strong Christian background. They were pagan and they worshiped pagan god, and every close tie with pagan worshiper.

Some of them claim they took the Ten Commandments from Deuteronomy. That doesn't make sense. How come they did not see Exodus? How come they did not compare them? Why didn't they teach the first and second commandments as one? How come? Why are they teaching women not to covet your neighbor's wife? If that is a separate commandment, what is the verse for it? What is the verse for the next commandments?

Division of the Ten Commandments by Religion/Denomination

Commandment	Jewish	Anglican, Reformed, and other Christians	Orthodox	Roman Catholics, Lutheran**
I am the Lord your God.	1	preface	1	1
You shall have no other Gods before me.	2	1	1	1
You shall not make for yourself an idol.	2	2	2	1
You shall not make wrongful use of the name of your God.	3	3	3	2
Remember the Sabbath and keep it holy.	4	4	4	3
Honor your father and mother.	5	5	5	4
You shall not murder.*	6	6	6	5
You shall not commit adultery.	7	7	7	6
You shall not steal.***	8	8	8	7
You shall not bear false witness against your neighbor.	9	9	9	8
You shall not covet your neighbor's house.	10	10	10	9
You shall not covet your neighbor's wife.	10	10	10	10

Once again, the Ten Commandments discuss neighbors. They do not understand why there is a law or a commandment. They are misleading the people and letting them enter into sin. They took the Ten Commandments from the Bible and used it for their convenience. They did not want people to understand them according to the Bible. They make people disagree with the Bible. Why are they doing this?

If anyone makes the wrong choice, they will never reach the destination. If anyone wants to go Niagara Falls—but goes east instead of west—no matter how long they drive, they will never reach Niagara Falls. Isn't it wise to buy a map and use it? It will help and be useful to travel a path. Will they know whether they are going the right direction? Will it make them more confident in their destination?

Remember no one serves two masters. Please God. Serving a religion is not the same as serving God. God is perfect. Religion is not perfect. Do not think they are making mistakes—they are sinning. They know who to serve.

"He who belongs to God hears what God says. The reason you do not hear is that you do not belong to God" (John 8:47).

CHAPTER 14

WHY READ THE BIBLE?

Jesus answered them, "You are wrong because you know neither the
scriptures nor the power of God."
—Matt. 22:29

Why should you read the Bible? God wanted Isaiah to tell people they should seek and read the Bible. These are the words of God. Jesus said the same thing.

Many people in the Christian community are not encouraging others to read the Bible. In fact, they are discouraging others from reading the Bible. That is why this chapter is important and deals with basic ideas. Many people were discouraged from reading the Bible in Christianity. It is not because God wants you not to read the Bible. It used to be in churches. Now regular people do not want you to read the Bible.

In today's world, there are many groups and many doctrines. Many people discourage people not to read the Bible. They point out that there are so many doctrines. Those people are right. There are many groups and different doctrines. However, they are not wrong in everything.

They do make mistakes—and some of their doctrines are wrong. People make mistakes. Also, there are people who act like believers in doctrines based on Bible verses. No one has the right to discourage you from reading the Bible.

There was a time when churches did not want people to read the Bible. However, in today's world every church wants you to read the Bible. I would not talk about the dark side of church history. Whatever it is, you need to understand who wants you to read the Bible. Isaiah does not want you to read scriptures. God wants his people to read his book. Since God wants you to read his scripture, why do you bother listening to others? If they are discouraging you from reading, they are against God—and against common sense. If you do not have common sense, you cannot even read a newspaper.

You have to choose who your God is. Is the one that discourages you a god? Or is God is your god? People act like saviors until you ask them for money. When you ask them for money, they want you to be independent. Even if they give you money, they want it back. When they advise you, they want you to keep their advice. You have the right to repay their advice. Many people would say you need the Holy Spirit to read the Bible. Knowledge of God is a gift of the Holy Spirit. Understanding is a gift of the Holy Spirit. If you do not hear or read something, how can you understand it? How can you have knowledge about it?

Who would have a completely wrong idea about God and scripture? "You are wrong because you know neither the scriptures nor the power of God" (Matt. 22:29). You may not notice—even if you are a regular Bible reader. You may wonder if it is really in the Bible. Yes, it is in the Bible. Why is this verse invisible to many readers? It is invisible because it comes from the middle of a discussion with the Sadducees. The Sadducees were a Jewish group in Jesus's time. The Sadducees questioned Jesus on human resurrection. Jesus told them why they had the wrong ideas. Jesus told them their ideas were wrong because they lacked knowledge of scripture. In other words, Jesus was asking them to read and understand scripture.

Jesus was not against scribes or phrases. If someone speaks against a cab who takes bribes, it does not mean they are against cabs. Good cabs hate cabs who take bribes. It does not mean they are against cabs and law and order. They are against cabs with bad behavior. They are against dishonesty. It does not mean they ignore the importance of policing.

If someone speaks negatively about someone or some group, it is the other side of the coin. It has good side. The negative side is discussed only to get rid of it. For example, if someone told you not to think about using a knife for killing, are they telling you to not use the knife for cooking? Without cooking, you would starve to death. God wants prophets to write and speak. If you want to get close to God, read it because that is what God wants. God wants his prophets to write down the reasons. You may be the reason.

There are many doctrines; which I should follow? "All the children shall be taught by the Lord, and great shall be the prosperity of your children" (Isa. 53:13).

If you read the Bible carefully, it says God will teach you. "And they shall all be taught by God. Everyone who has heard and learned from the Father comes to me" (John 6:45). God wants to teach you, and God wants you to have knowledge of him. How? (God) "desires steadfast love and not sacrifice, the knowledge of God rather than burnt offerings" (Hos. 6:6).

Many preach that you need to have faith. They won't say you need to have knowledge and faith. Since both are gifts of the Holy Spirit, you need to have both. Why do Christians preach about faith and ignore the subject of knowledge? If you have the faith, do not say a word. They want people to know they need to have faith. Without the knowledge of God, they would not know that. They cannot preach to those who do not have the knowledge of faith. Paul wrote about faith. Why did he write it?

He wanted people to have faith. In other words, he wanted them to have knowledge of faith. Without knowledge of God, faith loses its potency.

If people do not act upon faith, it is useless. This is also in the Bible. People who do not have faith won't do any work for Jesus. Action becomes the final stage of faith. Action stands on faith. Action becomes the focal point. If you read it, you will know action is the final stage of faith. Faith stands on knowledge. They are unbreakable and important. If you take one away, the other one dies by itself. And then there is no Christianity.

Why does today's Christianity focus only on faith? There were many groups in the second stage of early Christianity. Those who believed in knowledge or inner knowledge were called Gnostics in the second stage of early Christianity. In the third stage of early Christianity—when they became political—Roman kings did not approve of them. Knowledge of God disappeared in Christianity. It is important to understand God will give the Holy Spirit and lead you from inside. If your children dream, your children will prophesize. It is inner knowledge. Some evangelical preachers claim to hear the voice of the Holy Spirit. I am not trying to support Gnostics. God wants you to have knowledge of him rather than your offerings. Since I am coding Hosea 6:6 "God wants you to have the knowledge of him" knowledge of god became subject of faith.

Knowledge of God is important for prayer. (Faith is important too). Every Christian prayer may be blasphemous. To ignore them, you need to have knowledge of their beliefs and what is right to believe. If you have knowledge of God, you avoid praying with them. Nova's individual obedience was as important to God as other disobedient people ignoring the words of God. Quality is more important than quantity. Of course, a lot of good quality is even better.

Why have some sections of the Bible been corrupted? "We are wise, and the law of the Lord is with us, when in fact, the false pen of the scribes has made it into a lie" (Jer. 8:8). God told Jeremiah that religious leaders or writers wrote false statements about law and scripture. It was for Jewish people. It was not for anyone else. It already started to happen 2,600 years ago.

Religious leaders had some involvement in politics in part of history. They led the people toward political situations. Most of the time, they falsely used the Word of God to get people's support. In the worst cases, they added, removed, edited, and changed verse in a lot of sections of the Bible.

There are corrupted (tares) verses in the Bible. Some of them have been removed by churches. John 1:5:7 is different in different versions of the Bible. Unfortunately, there is more corruption. Even speaking out about it will put basic religious beliefs in trouble. There are mistakes in the Bible because of selfish political motives—not because of prophets or God.

> If anyone adds to them—God will add to that a person a plague described in this book. If anyone takes away from the words the book of this prophecy—God will take away that person's share in the tree of life. (Rev. 22:18-19)

This warning for Christians proves there are people in the Christian community who added or removed verses. This was not a warning for gentiles or pagans. It was a warning for their own kind. It proves the spirit of the wicked one will even try to corrupt a prophecy. Despite the warnings, someone may have added some words to Revelations.

That is why the Holy Spirit leads you toward the truth. That is why Christianity does not completely rely on books. That is why you need to receive the Holy Spirit. Jesus did not promise a book would guide you. Jesus said the Spirit of the Father would guide you. If God wants you to follow a book completely, receiving the Holy Spirit doesn't make any sense.

Christianity completely relies on the Holy Spirit. Jesus said it would lead us in truth. Scriptures are part of how the Holy Spirit works. Understanding is the gift of the Holy Spirit.

Many preachers say you need to believe in the Bible 100 percent. However, they may never point out any verses to support it. The Bible asks us to completely rely on the Holy Spirit but the Bible never asks us to completely rely on scriptures. The Bible warns us the scriptures would be corrupted. The corrupted verses can be identified if you have received the Holy Spirit.

> Seek and read from the book of the Lord: Not one of these shall be missing; none shall be without its mate. For the mouth of the Lord has commanded, and his spirit has gathered them. (Isa. 34:16)